Australia

This book presents a concise, up-to-date story of the people, history, geography, economy and culture of our country and its relations with the world. *Australia* has been prepared by Overseas Information Branch, Department of Foreign Affairs and Trade, and succeeds *Australia Handbook,* the 24th edition of which was published in 1986. The help received from Australian government departments, associated organisations and other authorities is gratefully acknowledged. Money values are in Australian currency; weights and measures are metric. Unless otherwise indicated, information is current to 31 January, 1990.

4

An Overseas Information Branch, Department of Foreign Affairs and Trade publication, published by the Australian Government Publishing Service, Canberra, 1990

(Cover) Aboriginal artist, Darby Jampijinja Ross, at Jukayuka, an area west of Yuendumu, Northern Territory. Darby is custodian of this area.

Editor: Brian R. Cummins

Designer: John Simpson

Printed in Australia by Finepress Offset Printing Pty. Ltd. Auburn N.S.W.

ISBN 0 644 09784 1

Metric equivalents

Mass

1 gram	*0.0353 ounce*	*g*
1 kilogram	*2.20 pounds*	*kg*
1 tonne	*0.984 ton*	*t*

Volume

1 litre	*1.76 pints*	*L*
1 megalitre	*219 969 gallons*	*ML*
1 cubic metre	*35.3 cubic feet*	m^3

Temperature

0 degrees Celsius	*32 degrees Fahrenheit*	
0_C	0_F	

Length

1 millimetre	*0.0394 inch*	*mm*
1 centimetre	*0.394 inch*	*cm*
1 metre	*3.28 feet or 1.09 yards*	*m*
1 kilometre	*0.621 mile*	*km*

Area

1 square metre	*10.8 square feet*	m^2
1 hectare	*2.47 acres*	*ha*
1 square km	*0.386*	km^2

Contents

East Macdonnell Ranges, Northern Territory

Australia — an outline

When one of Australia's authors dubbed his homeland 'the lucky country' he was right in many respects, but its luck has not been unmixed. Its isolation over millenniums gave it many advantages but its size and its low, erratic water supplies counter them.

The way its people have met their country's challenges is outlined in this booklet.

The world's smallest continent and largest island, Australia was once part of prehistoric Gondwanaland, which divided into Africa, India, South America, Antarctica and the Great South Land.

A land 'bridge' between Australia and Asia may have provided access 40 000 years ago for Australia's first immigrants, the Aboriginals. They were its sole inhabitants until two centuries ago.

Indonesian traders probably visited Australia's north-west but it was unknown to the rest of the world until the 1600s. A huge south land appeared on maps before 200 AD but its existence was not confirmed until the 17th century when Portuguese, Spanish and Dutch merchants ventured into Asia.

The first European settlement of the continent — by the British — began in 1788, on the site now occupied by Sydney, Australia's largest city.

There were then about 1500 Europeans and perhaps 300 000 Aboriginals in Australia. The population had reached 2.25 million by 1881, 5.44 million by 1921 and 7.4 million by the end of World War II (1945). It increased sharply, partly because of a large postwar immigration program, and reached 16 million in the late 1980s, despite a decline that began in the 1970s in natural increase and net immigration. The rate of population increase in the 40 years after World War II, about two per cent, has halved.

The scale of the immigration program became large in the late 1940s and, in the ensuing four decades, more than four million people from 120-plus countries settled in Australia. Britain and Ireland contributed 1.79 million and 1.5 million came from Italy, Greece, Yugoslavia, The Netherlands, Germany, New Zealand, Poland, the US, Vietnam and Lebanon. Australia has become a multicultural society.

Australia has a land area of 7 682 300km² and its coastline is 36 735km long. It is the world's driest inhabited continent; vast areas are arid or semi-desert, and virtually uninhabited. Most of its population lives on the coastal fringe.

Ranking about 20th in the world in the value of its overseas trade, Australia exports goods worth more than $40 000 million each year and imports goods to much the same value.

Its population has a high standard of living by world standards and most families own or are buying their own houses.

Its flag is the only one to fly over a whole continent. Until Australia's six colonies federated in 1901, Britain's Union Jack was its official flag but the new nation chose a new design. It has a blue field with the Union Jack in the canton (the upper quarter next to the flagpole). The seven-pointed star in the lower hoist represents the states and territories. In the fly are the five stars of the constellation Southern Cross.

Australia's national anthem is a revised version of a late 19th-century patriotic song, *Advance Australia Fair*. The words are:

Australians all let us rejoice,
For we are young and free;
We've golden soil and wealth for toil;
Our home is girt by sea;
Our land abounds in nature's gifts
Of beauty rich and rare;
In history's page, let every stage
Advance Australia Fair.
In joyful strains then let us sing,
Advance Australia Fair.

Beneath our radiant Southern Cross
We'll toil with hearts and hands;
To make this Commonwealth of ours
Renowned of all the lands;
For those who've come across the seas
We've boundless plains to share;
With courage let us all combine
To Advance Australia Fair.
In joyful strains then let us sing,
Advance Australia Fair.

The anthem is used on all official and ceremonial occasions. It became the anthem in 1984, replacing *God Save the Queen*, known since then as the royal anthem. Both anthems are played on royal occasions.

Australia's coat of arms is a shield containing the badges of the six states, enclosed by an ermine border signifying federation. The crest is a seven- pointed gold star on a blue and gold wreath. The supporters are Australian fauna — a kangaroo and an emu. Usually the arms are depicted with an adornment (not part of the arms) of wattle and a scroll bearing the word 'Australia' under the arms.

Although Australia has never adopted formally any official motto or floral, faunal or bird emblem, the motto 'Advance Australia' appeared for many years on unofficial coats of arms, even before federation. By tradition, the golden wattle, kangaroo and emu are widely regarded as national floral, faunal and bird emblems.

Green and gold have been used traditionally by Australian Olympic and other sporting teams for most of the 20th century but they did not become the national colours formally until 1984.

Australia has no official or traditional national costume.

The official language is English — by usage, not law. It has its own colloquialisms and slang but does not differ importantly from the modern mother tongue or the English spoken elsewhere, except in accent. Spelling generally follows the British form.

January 26, the date of the first European settlement of the continent in 1788, is Australia's national day.

Of the other days observed nationally in Australia, two evoke great fervour and throw a curious sidelight on the national character:
• Anzac Day, April 25, on which Australians honour their war dead and those who fought and survived. The date chosen is the anniversary of the greatest military defeat Australia has suffered.
• The first Tuesday in November, when Australia's world-famous horse race, the Melbourne Cup, is run. In its home city, Melbourne, it is a holiday; and all work ceases across the nation while the race is run.

International relations

Well into the 20th century, Australia's ethnic background was overwhelmingly English and Irish and many of its citizens still called the British Isles 'home'.

As the 21st century draws near, 'home' to most Australians is Australia and 'the old country' for those actually born elsewhere might be of more than a hundred parts of the world.

Furthermore, despite Australia's western traditions and orientation, it is geographically part of South-East Asia and is a middle-level world power.

As the Minister for Foreign Affairs and Trade, Senator Gareth Evans, said in his address to the Australian National University's Strategic and Defence Studies Centre Bicentennial Conference in Canberra on 6 December 1988, Australia's national interests can be divided into three groups:

- geopolitical and strategic interests in defence of Australian sovereignty and political independence;
- economic and trade interests; and
- those interests involved in being a good international citizen.

Australia's relationships with Britain, the US and Western Europe, forged by history, are important factors in Australian policy. However, its growing awareness of the importance of the politically, economically and strategically significant countries of Asia and the many newly independent nations of the South Pacific has led Australia to foster friendly and cooperative relations with them. Australia is keen to ensure the stability and security of the region and to develop mutually profitable trade, investment, technological exchanges and cooperation in development.

Relations with China, Japan, ASEAN (the Association of South-East Asian Nations), New Zealand, Papua New Guinea and other South Pacific states are of significance to Australia. Similarly, in the Indian Ocean, Australia has important political, strategic and economic interests and observes and considers carefully the issues of the region. This is true particularly in the development of relations with the ocean's island states, including Mauritius, Madagascar and the Maldives, and with East African states.

Australia pursues issues internationally that reflect its people's attitudes and concerns: disarmament, the plight of refugees, human rights, the easing of East-West tension, the abolition of chemical weapons and international trade liberalisation.

It has developed constructive, progressive policies and has assumed a practical and active posture in the pursuit of world peace. It has become a leader in the movement toward a comprehensive nuclear test ban treaty and has long maintained an Ambassador for Disarmament.

The United Nations has had no more consistent supporter than Australia for its charter and the work of its specialised agencies. It participates in many UN activities and has served on many of its bodies, including the Security Council.

Among the specialised agencies and subsidiary bodies Australia supports are those assisting in development, food security, children, drug control and human rights. It has served for a number of years on the Commission on Human Rights, has provided money, personnel and equipment for almost all major UN peacekeeping activities, contributes its assessed share of the costs of all UN operations and makes additional contributions. It is fully involved in UN disarmament, arms control and outer space work. Australia accepts the jurisdiction of the International Court of Justice and is active in the development of international law. It has been a member of the Organisation for Economic Cooperation and Development (OECD) since 1971.

The Commonwealth of Nations brings together about a quarter of the world's population and Australia takes part in the broad range of its activities.

The growing interdependence of economic and foreign policy, Australia's increasing dependence on international trade and the effects of world economic conditions on its domestic economy has led to a sharpened focus on international trade issues in the pursuit of its foreign policy.

Australia's economic and political future is linked closely with those of its Asian and other Pacific neighbours.

Progress made by ASEAN and its contribution to regional cooperation are sources of satisfaction to Australia, which has an interest in helping to ensure ASEAN's success in generating economic growth and political stability. Australia has a program of economic cooperation with ASEAN through which it supports important regional projects. It also contributes significantly toward easing the burden of Indo-Chinese refugees in member countries.

Australia takes the view that peace and prosperity in the Asia-Pacific region depend on the ability of the region's countries to cooperate to maintain economic growth and political stability. Such cooperation, it believes, ensures that no major power, regional or otherwise, can exert undue influence. Australia has long involved itself, therefore, in regional organisations such as the UN Economic and Social Commissions for Asia and the Pacific, the Colombo Plan and the Asian Development Bank.

Japan is Australia's largest trading partner and relations are based on complementary interests and shared perceptions of international issues. Cultural, scientific, sporting and other relations are fostered by both to improve mutual understanding.

Australia's relations with China have been marked since diplomatic links were established in 1972 by regular, reciprocal, high-level visits. China is a significant market for Australia and the relationship is underpinned by agreements and institutional arrangments (culture, science and technology, agriculture, civil aviation, education, and the Australia-China Council). A technical cooperation program, designed to help China's development, includes activities in education, energy, forestry, health and industrial technology.

As a result of the 1989 Tiananmen Square massacre and the suppression of the pro-democracy movement in China, the Australian Government reviewed carefully its relationship with China.

Australia's relationship with the Republic of Korea has developed significantly in recent years. Korea has emerged as a major economic power in its region and has become one of Australia's more important trading partners.

Friendly relations, including development assistance programs, exist with Myanmar (formerly Burma) and Laos, and a constructive political dialogue with Vietnam has developed. This has been important to Australia's efforts to seek a just, lasting and peaceful settlement in Cambodia.

In the Pacific region, Australia promotes stability, welfare and economic development. It has friendly relations with the island countries in the South and Central Pacific and has a number of diplomatic missions in the area. Its aid programs in the region cover all aspects of social and economic life in those countries.

History has created a special and close relationship between Australia and Papua New Guinea. Since Papua New Guinea achieved independence in 1975 the relationship has encompassed a broad range of government and non-government activities.

As a foundation member of the South Pacific Commission, the South Pacific Forum and the South Pacific convention which established the Forum Fisheries Agency, Australia takes an active part in them and in many other regional forums on a broad range of issues, including development of an environmental protection convention. It provides substantial financial support for programs developed in the South Pacific, such as the South Pacific Regional Environment Program, a regional network of climate-monitoring stations and the Regional Civil Aviation Project, and it has established a fund to preserve and develop Pacific cultures. With New Zealand it has entered a non-reciprocal preferential trade agreement in favour of South Pacific Forum states — the South Pacific Regional Trade and Economic Cooperation Agreement (SPARTECA).

It has a close relationship with New Zealand. The 1983 Australia New Zealand Closer Economic Relations Trade Agreement aims to remove barriers to trans-Tasman trade.

There has long been a close relationship with the United States. Government-to-government relations are only part of an interaction born of common experiences, culture and language. The US is an important trading partner despite the development in recent years of differences between the two over trade policies, particularly as they affect agriculture.

Canada is closely comparable to Australia in its history, institutions, traditions, land area, economic standing and international outlook. The goodwill between the two allows them to cooperate on a range of objectives without affecting individual national interests or commercial competition.

Australia is concerned at the debt problems of Latin America and the Caribbean region, the human-rights records of some Latin American governments and tensions in Central America. It has supported efforts to find peaceful solutions to these problems.

Friendly relations with Western European countries and the European Community (EC) are of considerable importance to Australia. Bilateral relations with individual Western European countries are based on shared cultural and historical links and reinforced by the presence in Australia of large numbers of their former citizens and by significant economic ties.

The EC is an important trading partner and a major source of investment funds and scientific and technological expertise.

Australia has a keen interest in a balanced East-West relationship. It has diplomatic contacts with the Soviet Union and Eastern Europe. Eastern European markets have significant potential for Australian exports, particularly commodities, and trade relations have been expanding. In Australia, large ethnic groups from Eastern Europe have substantial links, notably cultural, with their countries of origin.

The value Australia places on its long-standing relations with the Arab nations and Israel is high. It supports the efforts of parties to the Middle East dispute to find a just, lasting and peaceful solution, although its ability to influence settlement is limited. Australian trade with the region's countries is significant.

Australia pursues friendly relations with independent African states. It has formal relations with South Africa but has been prominent in opposing apartheid and has actively encouraged the process of transition to independence and self-government in Namibia. Australian assistance to African countries includes project support, food aid and training. Australia has always moved quickly and effectively to bring relief aid to the victims of disasters in Africa.

Nuclear policies in Australia are based on strong support of the Nuclear Non-Proliferation Treaty. Its policy on the sale of its uranium includes a condition that it will not be used for military or explosive purposes and that buyers accept International Atomic Energy Agency safeguards. Agreements have been signed with Britain, Canada, Egypt, the European Atomic Energy Community, Finland, France, Japan, the Philippines, the Republic of Korea, Sweden, Switzerland and the US.

Australia has been prominent in promoting the concept of a nuclear-free zone in the South Pacific.

Australia took part in the Law of the Sea Conference, the largest and potentially the most important conference in the history of the UN, involving major strategic, economic, transport, scientific and environmental issues.

Proximity and long association with Antarctica underpin its importance to Australia, which maintains three permanent bases in the Australian Antarctic Territory at Casey, Davis and Mawson. One of the original signatories to the Antarctic Treaty, Australia has important scientific, environmental and security interests there. It believes the Treaty system has kept Antarctica free from contention and provides the best means of managing Antarctica effectively in the future.

The Australian Government took a leading role in efforts to have Antarctica declared a world park to protect its fragile environment.

The Department of Foreign Affairs and Trade conducts an overseas cultural exchange program in cooperation with the Australia Council and other cultural bodies. The program includes the performing and visual arts, film-making, literature, and academic and sporting exchanges. Australia has cultural agreements with China, France, Greece, India, Indonesia, Iran, Italy, Japan, the Republic of Korea, Malaysia, the Philippines, Romania, Singapore, Thailand, Yugoslavia, and the Soviet Union.

Australia's overseas aid program aims to promote economic growth and social advancement in developing countries. All of Australia's aid (more than $1000 million a year in recent years) is given in grant form.

Papua New Guinea is the main recipient of Australian aid as budget support.

Aid to other countries is tied to specific development projects and its major recipients are the developing countries of South-East Asia and the South Pacific. Australia supports development programs in about 40 countries, ranging from large rural projects to village-level activities.

Countries in South Asia and Africa and Indian Ocean states also receive Australian help. Programs in these areas are aimed at the rural poor. Food security, clean water, improved animal husbandry, rural infrastructure and transport projects are supported.

One of the world's largest providers of food aid to developing countries, Australia is committed to supplying 350 000 tonnes of wheat, or its equivalent, each year. Most of this aid goes to African countries facing particularly severe food shortages, or countries (such as Bangladesh or Pakistan) with emergency needs resulting from severe crop failure, natural disasters, or refugee flows. Direct food support is complemented by programs aimed at improving longer-term food security.

Australia contributes to the education of about 18 000 students from developing countries, mostly at tertiary level. The Australian International Development Assistance Bureau (AIDAB) pays about $80 million a year to subsidise this program. A new education policy based on merit and equity is providing more opportunities for students from poorer and isolated developing countries.

A major part of Australia's support for the education of foreign students is the full cost of studies for about 1000 of them and support for the Australian Universities International Development Program.

Non-government organisations, including the International Red Cross, contribute significantly to Australia's aid effort and the Government supports their activities, including programs under which Australian volunteers work in developing countries.

The Australian Centre for International Agricultural Research supports research into the agricultural problems of developing-countries. It commissions research by Australian agricultural institutions in partnership with developing country research groups. The main beneficiaries of the research are Australia's near neighbours in South-East Asia, the South Pacific and Papua New Guinea.

Environment

The wellbeing of the environment was for decades the concern of the few. They, dedicated to halting what they realised was a potentially catastrophic neglect, waste or destruction of the globe's resources and recovery mechanisms, became 'radicals'. But because they were right, the majority came to accept their cause as just and, later, that their air of urgency was justified. Australia was neither slower nor quicker than other industrialised nations to come to that realisation.

Having done so, however, Australia has moved to the vanguard of nations that have accepted their responsibility and taken action to halt and, where feasible, reverse the effects of all three.

Australia has been concentrating on key environmental issues such as soil erosion, landscape-quality preservation, water-quality improvement, chemicals control, including hazardous-waste handling and disposal, "greenhouse-effect" climatic change, depletion of the ozone layer, assessment of the impact of the full range of human activity on the environment and the preservation of the nation's heritage.

All levels of government are involved in and responsible for the multitude of Australian concerns in environmental matters. The Federal Government assigns responsibility for its role to a Minister and a department, commonly one with other responsibilities having a bearing on those concerns.

Australia was one of the first countries to ratify the World Heritage Convention, the aim of which is to promote co-operation among nations to protect those things of such universal value that their conservation is of concern to all people.

It is the only country to have enacted legislation specifically to carry out its responsibilities under the convention: the World Heritage Properties Conservation Act 1983.

On a national level, it has established the Australian Heritage Commission, one of the main functions of which is the preparation and maintenance of a Register of the National Estate.

This register lists all parts of Australia's natural, historic and Aboriginal heritage that should be kept for future generations.

Well over 8 000 such places are on the register.

The main federal program backing this commitment to preserving Australia's heritage is the National Estate Grants Program, established in 1983 to provide financial assistance to serious efforts to preserve it. More than 3000 grants have been made to state and territory governments and conservation bodies under this program.

The specific spheres of concern under the general heading of the environment are so numerous that, while they require mention, their treatment in a document of this type must be confined to a simple list — although notes on some of the more prominent subjects are necessary. These subjects include: land use, Antarctica, coastal management, the sea, forests, unspoiled areas, mining, primary industries, tourism, bushfires, wetlands, endangered species, land degradation,

Rainforest, southwest Tasmania

soil salinity, dumping of wastes at sea, sea installations, the great barrier reef, the greenhouse effect, marine matters generally, flora and fauna, trees, specifically rainforests, specifically, hazardous chemicals, specifically agricultural chemicals, the ozone layer, recycling of all forms of waste, ionising radiation, noise, lead and other heavy metals, air quality, national parks.

All Australian states have legislation or procedural arrangements to provide for environmental factors to be taken into account in decision-making, particularly when land development or industrial activities are involved. The federal and state governments have agreements for cooperative environmental assessments.

Uranium mining proceeds only under the most rigid controls and in a severely limited set of circumstances. Sales of uranium are controlled even more rigidly; details appear elsewhere in this booklet.

Virtually all of the Great Barrier Reef is part of a marine national park.

Water-lilies, Lake Waggaboonyah, Queensland

The Federal Government regulates dumping of wastes at sea in accordance with the London Dumping Convention. In collaboration with state authorities, it has a national air-quality program which collects and analyses data.

The first laws to protect scenic areas in Australia were passed in Tasmania in 1863. In 1879, the Royal National Park of 7284ha was established south of Sydney. This was Australia's first national park, and the world's second.

Now more than 40 million ha, or a twentieth of Australia's total land area, is reserved for national parks and other types of conservation reserves. Australia now has more than 2000 national parks, conservation parks, reserves and refuges and the area set aside for conservation is increasing. National parks and wildlife services exist in all states to manage state national parks and reserves.

Native fauna in Australia are protected and managed by state and territorial governments, while the Federal Government's concern is mainly the control of international import and export, international treaties and conventions pertaining to nature conservation.

Australia's approach to kangaroo conservation and management has two main objectives — to maintain populations of kangaroos over their natural range and at the same time to contain their harmful effects on other land-management practices.

Legislation passed in 1981 prohibits killing, capturing, injuring or interfering with a whale, dolphin or porpoise in the 200-mile Australian fishing zone and by Australian vessels and aircraft beyond the 200-mile zone.

States and Territories

Australia has six States: New South Wales (NSW), Victoria (Vic), Queensland (Qld), South Australia (SA), Western Australia (WA) and Tasmania (Tas). It also has three internal Territories (the Northern Territory (NT), the Australian Capital Territory (ACT) which includes the Jervis Bay Territory and seven external Territories.

The external Territories are: Norfolk Island; the uninhabited Coral Sea Islands in the Pacific Ocean; the Cocos (Keeling) Islands; Christmas Island; the uninhabited Ashmore and Cartier Islands Territory in the Indian Ocean; the Territory of Heard Island and the McDonald Islands in the sub-Antarctic; and the Australian Antarctic Territory.

NSW, in the south-east, was the first colony Britain established in Australia and is now the most populous (nearly six million) and heavily industrialised state in Australia. It is highly urbanised. Sydney, its capital, is Australia's largest city (population more than 3.5 million) and one of the world's great seaports.

Agricultural and pastoral industries, broadly based manufacturing, ample energy raw materials and highly developed service industries are the basis of its economy.

South of NSW, Victoria drew its first permanent European settlers from its island sister colony, Tasmania, attracted by the rich soil and grasslands. The nucleus of Melbourne, its capital, was established in 1835. Victoria's population is approaching 4.5 million, of whom a little more than three million live in Melbourne.

Its economy is based on agricultural and pastoral industries (it produces about a quarter of Australia's rural output), secure energy resources, a broadly based manufacturing sector and highly developed service industries.

European settlement in Queensland began in 1824 when a group of convicts and their guards landed near the mouth of the Brisbane River to begin a penal settlement. Free settlement began in earnest in 1842.

Sunset on Sydney Harbour

The second-largest State in area and the third-most-populous, it has nearly three million inhabitants, of whom more than a million live in Brisbane, the capital. Queensland accounts for a fifth of Australia's agricultural and mining production and about a quarter of the value of its exports.

South Australia was founded in 1836 by the London-based South Australian Company. Among its pioneers were Germans, victims of religious persecution, who began to arrive about three years later.

It has an area of 984 000km^2 and a population of about 1.5 million, of whom just over a million live in Adelaide, the capital.

For its first century the State survived mainly on agriculture. Such produce is still its most important export (though its climate limits agriculture to a tenth of its area) and represents about a third of Australia's agricultural exports. In the last 40 years secondary industry has come to employ three times as many people — a fifth of its workforce.

In 1829, the British sea captain James Stirling established a colony, now called Perth, on the banks of the Swan River in the south-west corner of the continent. By 1989, Perth's population had grown to more than a million and that of the State, Western Australia, to about one and a half million. Its area, a third of the continent, is 2 525 500km^2 and its coastline 12 500km.

Its mineral wealth is enormous and, although it has only a twelfth of Australia's population, WA accounts because of its mineral exports for about a quarter of its income.

The first major mineral discovery, in the 1890s, was gold, which it still produces. It has become the largest diamond-producing state in the world and has developed rich mines of iron, nickel, bauxite-alumina, uranium, oil and natural gas, mineral sands, coal, salt, copper and other minerals. Iron ore is its biggest income earner.

Its farm production is mainly wheat and sheep.

Tasmania, the smallest State (68 331km^2), is an island about 240km south of the mainland's south-east corner. The capital, Hobart, was established in 1803.

About 40 per cent of its population (approaching 500 000) lives in and around Hobart.

Farms cover a third of its area but it also has more than 500 factories producing foodstuffs, textiles, clothing, footwear, wood and paper products, chemicals, metals, transport equipment, industrial machinery and household appliances. By turnover, its major industries are foodstuffs, basic metals, paper and wood, wood products and textiles.

When the States federated at the turn of the century they wrote into the Constitution that there would be a national capital on federal territory. In 1911, 2359km^2 of land 320km south-west of Sydney was designated Australian Capital Territory (ACT).

The national capital, Canberra, was built in the ACT and its population is approaching 300 000. More than half its wage and salary earners are employed by government departments or agencies. Until 1989, when it achieved limited self-government, the ACT had been administered by the Federal Government. In March 1989, it elected a

Melbourne, capital of the State of Victoria, a business, cultural and sporting centre

17-member House of Assembly which has powers far beyond those of a city council but not as wide as those of a sovereign State. The Australian Capital Territory elects two members to the House of Representatives and two Senators.

The Territory of Jervis Bay, on the NSW coast east of Canberra, occupies 7360ha, two-thirds of it a declared public park. Administratively it is part of the ACT and satisfies a constitutional requirement that the ACT have "access to the sea".

The Northern Territory covers 1 346 200km^2 — nearly a fifth of the continent. More than twice the size of France and as far from north to south as London to Lisbon or New York to Miami, most of it is in the tropics.

It achieved limited self-government in 1978. The areas of responsibility transferred from the Federal Government, and its powers within them, are much the same as those enjoyed by the states. There is an administrator instead of a governor and a chief minister instead of a premier.

The Territory's parliament is the Legislative Assembly, of 25 members elected for a four-year term.

Mining is the territory's main industry, the most important products being uranium, manganese, copper, gold, bismuth and bauxite. Others are tin, silver, lead and zinc. Second to mining is tourism, which is growing rapidly. Beef cattle production is a major rural industry. Agriculture has been diversifying in recent years.

Norfolk Island, 1676km east-north-east of Sydney, became a Territory of Australia in 1914. Originally a convict settlement, established in 1788 (the same year as Australia's first colony), it was abandoned in 1814 and resettled in 1825. The last convicts were removed in 1855. Accepting an offer made to them by Queen Victoria of England, 194 descendants of the mutineers of the Bounty were taken from Pitcairn Island to Norfolk Island in 1856. Today their descendants number half the permanent population of about 1400.

In 1979, Norfolk Island achieved elected, responsible legislative and executive government, and runs its own affairs to the greatest practicable extent by the Legislative Assembly and by an Executive Council comprising the executive members of the Legislative Assembly, who have ministerial-type responsibilities.

The Territory of Cocos (Keeling) Islands lies in the Indian Ocean, 2768km north-west of Perth. Twenty-seven coral islands, forming two atolls, make up the territory and have a combined land area of 14km².

The islands are believed to have been discovered in 1609 by Captain William Keeling of the British East India Company. The first permanent settlement was established in 1826 on the main atoll by an Englishman, Alexander Hare. In 1827, Captain John Clunies-Ross, a Scottish seaman and business associate of Hare, formed a second settlement to which be brought Malay labourers. The islands were inadvertently declared part of the British dominions in 1857 by Captain Stephen Grenville Fremantle. In 1886, Queen Victoria granted all land on the islands to George Clunies-Ross and his heirs in perpetuity, subject to future Crown requirements. By mutual agreement between the British

Central business district of Perth, capital of Western Australia

and Australian governments confirmed by complementary legislation in 1955, the islands became an Australian territory. In 1978, the Australian Government bought Mr John Clunies-Ross's interests in the islands except for his residence and associated buildings.

About 600 people live in the Territory. Nearly all 400-plus permanent residents are descendants of the people, predominantly Malays, brought to the islands by Hare and Clunies-Ross as indentured labour. With few exceptions, Cocos Malays living there are now Australian citizens.

In 1984, in a United Nations-observed Act of Self-Determination, the Cocos-Malay community voted for integration with Australia. The Australian Government is represented by an Administrator.

The Coral Sea Islands Territory, a group of islands scattered over about 780 000km² east of the Great Barrier Reef, are uninhabited except for a manned weather station on Willis Island. Automatic lighthouses and weather stations operate on other islands, most of which are breeding grounds for sea birds. Australia asserted its sovereignty over them in 1969.

The Ashmore and Cartier Islands Territory's four uninhabited islets are 350km north-west of Western Australia's coast. Ashmore Reef was declared a national nature reserve in 1983.

The 135km² Territory of Christmas Island is in the Indian Ocean 2623km north-west of Perth. The island was uninhabited until annexed by Britain in 1888 after the discovery of phosphate rock there. After phosphate mining ceased in 1984, more than half the inhabitants resettled, some in Singapore and most of the rest in Australia. Most of its 1300 present occupants are of Chinese or Malay origin. The Australian Government is represented by an Administrator.

The Government is pursuing the development of alternative industries for the island.

Australia has been active in research and exploration in the Antarctic since the early 1900s. British sovereignty, proclaimed by Sir Douglas Mawson during his 1929–31 expedition, was transferred later to Australia. Called the Australian Antarctic Territory (AAT), it covers 6.1 million km², more than two-fifths of the Antarctic continent, and includes all lands, except Terre Adelie, south of 60°S latitude and between 160° and 45°E longitudes.

Australia also has sub-Antarctic possessions — Macquarie Island and the Territory of Heard Island and the McDonald Islands.

Scientific programs in the AAT sub-Antarctic islands and Southern Ocean are carried out by various research organisations, one of which is a division of a Federal Government department. This division organises and supports the expeditions and stations — one on Macquarie Island and three (Casey, Davis and Mawson) on the Antarctic continent.

Australia is a signatory to the Antarctic Treaty and collaborates with other treaty parties in many of its scientific activities in the region. The Commission for the Conservation of Antarctic Marine Living Resources, established by the Antarctic Treaty parties in 1982, has its headquarters in Hobart.

Trade

Australia is a key supplier to the world of many important commodities; has a sound mix of exports; and has a generally solid balance of imports and exports.

The exports in which it leads the world are alumina, wool, beef and veal, coal, mineral sands, live sheep and goats and refined lead. Other important commodities of which it is a key supplier are wheat, sugar, iron ore, bauxite, nickel, and zinc and its ores.

A middle-level trading nation (about 20th in the world in value of imports and exports), Australia has seen a distinct change in the pattern of its international trade in the last quarter-century. Major trends have included a decline of the rural sector's share of total exports, from three-quarters to about a third, and an increase (from about a tenth to half) in that of the minerals, fuels and metals sector; a growth in Japan's importance as a trading partner and a decline in Britain's; and a deliberate and successful diversification, not only of range of products but of export markets, into the western Pacific region and the Middle East. Over all, Australia's trade is growing rapidly.

The relative decline of the rural sector's share of the export market masks the fact that it has grown in absolute terms, though more slowly than others. A major reason for sluggish growth has been its original heavy dependence on the slow-growing British market — and that market's decline when Britain joined the European Community — and a long-term fall in wool's share of the world textile market.

The diversification of Australia's products and markets has been achieved partly as a result of Australia's rapid economic and industrial growth and partly because of private-sector and government initiatives in export development programs and other promotional activity. Government participation includes trade missions at various levels, publicity campaigns, participation in trade fairs and the like.

The Australian Trade Commission (AUSTRADE) plays an important role in the development of the export trade by providing market intelligence, financial

Export coal at Newlands open-cut mine, Queensland.

and insurance support and employing a network of trade commissioners worldwide.

The manufacturing sector's share of overall exports grew strongly after World War II, reaching almost a quarter in the early 1970s. It declined steadily for a decade after that but vigorous encouragement since then has stabilised it at about a fifth.

Elaborately transformed manufactured products, in particular, account now for more than half the exports of manufactured goods.

The shifts in relative significance of Australia's trading partners has been substantial. Japan's role as a customer grew sharply from the early 1960s and, by the mid-1970s, it was buying a third of Australia's exports. Its share has stabilised at a little more than a quarter; it buys about a fifth of Australia's rural exports; two-fifths of its minerals, fuels and metals (including natural and manufactured gas); two-thirds of its iron ore and more than half of its coal.

At the same time Britain, having joined the EC, bought less of Australia's exports. The buyer of a tenth of those goods in the early 1970s, it now buys about a twenty-fifth. Developing countries, on the other hand, have become important to Australia, particularly those of South-East Asia. Such countries bought less than a fifth of Australia's exports in the 1950s but now account for more than a third.

Australia's import pattern is unusual for an industrialised country — it imports a lot of capital equipment and relatively little food, fuels and lubricants.

An important aspect of government involvement in trade has been its emphasis on developing Australia's manufacturing base and making it more competitive in the export field. This has included liberalisation of regulations and the gradual elimination of protective barriers, including tariffs. The result is that Australia has one of the lowest levels of across-the-board protection among the industrialised nations.

However, Australia still has a system of tariff preferences for developing countries, to help them compete on the Australian market against developed suppliers. It also gives advice to developing countries and those with centrally planned economies on how to market products in Australia.

Rough cut diamonds, a growing export item

Natural gas for overseas markets is carried in this giant tanker ship

America and Japan are Australia's largest suppliers of imports, accounting for about one fifth each. Britain, which supplied two-fifths of Australia's imported goods in the late 1950s, now sells it about a twentieth.

The developing countries' share of Australia's import market has grown from less than a sixth to nearly a quarter, largely because of the increase in petroleum imports.

Australia is committed to working for a fairer and more open world trading system, particularly in agricultural and natural-resource-based products.

Australia has two types of bilateral trade agreements. The first, preferential, provides for the exchange of special tariffs and other treatments which are not extended to third countries. The second, most-favoured-nation agreements, generally accord the same treatment to each other as to third countries. Australia's trade relations with most other major trading partners, including the US and the EC, are governed by common membership of GATT.

Under the 1983 Australia-New Zealand Closer Economic Relations trade agreement, tariffs on most goods traded across the Tasman began to phase down by at least five per cent a year, resulting in duty-free treatment for most goods by January 1, 1988. Provision has been made for the gradual liberalisation of import restrictions until they are eliminated by 1992.

L abour and industrial relations

The vast majority of Australians live and work in cities and towns and go to their workplaces by public transport or car. In the main they work seven to eight (daylight) hours a day, Monday to Friday, and take four weeks' paid leave a year — and many have a 17.5 per cent loading on their holiday pay.

The workforce is divided broadly into commercial (workers in shops, offices) and industrial (labour, services and factories). The former usually begin their working day at 8.30am to 9am and the latter between 7am and 8am, although many work in two or three shifts a day. The terminology is drifting now into disuse, but the commercial workers have been known for decades as white-collar workers and the industrial as blue-collar.

For more than a century, Australian women have been asserting their right of entry to virtually any occupation, more vigorously in recent years. Although their occupational profile is changing steadily, their numbers are still concentrated in teaching, nursing, clerical and sales jobs in the manufacturing, wholesale and retail trade and finance and business-services industries.

They constitute about two-fifths of the workforce; two-thirds are married.

Australia workers are highly unionised. The conciliation and arbitration system, which has encouraged this, operates on the premise that employers and employees will be represented before tribunals by registered organisations. About one in two employees belongs to Australia's 300-plus trade unions.

The main central organisation is the Australian Council of Trade Unions. It has an affiliated membership of more than 150 unions representing about three million workers.

The Confederation of Australian Industry has a membership of 35 employer organisations covering a wide range of industries. Its main objectives are to promote industry, trade and commerce and to encourage a united approach by employers to matters of common interest.

Working conditions are regulated by legislation and by industrial "awards", which have much the same function as collective agreements in other countries. The Constitution limits the power of the Australian Parliament in this sphere to legislation to prevent and settle (by conciliation and arbitration) industrial disputes extending beyond state limits. States, too, can regulate industrial relations, but do so only on matters within their own jurisdictions.

Federal legislation has established the Australian Industrial Relations Commission, which can intervene in interstate industrial disputes by request or of its own volition, and the Labour Court. The commission's members are arranged in panels, each to deal with disputes in a specific industry or group of industries.

If parties in dispute agree on settlement, they can ask the commission to certify the agreement or make an award giving it effect. Such agreements and 'consent' awards have the same effect as arbitral awards.

The Federal Government and all state governments have departments concerned with labour and industrial relations, which administer legislation which regulates safety and physical working conditions. Each state government has an industrial court or commission to hear state award matters and wages boards and tribunals to set general wage rates in industries for which they are responsible.

Federal and state tribunals set rates of pay (fixed without regard to the sex of the employee) and conditions of employment for seven out of eight Australian employees covered by awards, determinations or industrial agreements. Most are minimum rates, and employers often pay above-award rates.

In recent years, general pay increases have been given in return for unions' co-operation in restructuring and modernising their awards as part of a

Rest facilities for workers

program to encourage the development of skills.

The Racial Discrimination Act 1975 prohibits discrimination in employment on the grounds of race, colour, descent or national or ethnic origin.

An agreement, known nationally as the Accord, reached in 1983 between the Federal Government and the Australian Council of Trade Unions, established an agenda of reform and consultation in wage fixing. It is an integral part of the Government's economic policy.

In return for the unions' cooperation in implementing the Government's employment and anti-inflation policies, it undertook to help unions maintain their members' living standards and improve them over time.

Federal, state, and local governments employ about a quarter of the employed work force, excluding the Defence Force.

Australia's labour force is about two-thirds of the civilian population aged 15 or more. Four-fifths of the employed labour force works full-time and about half of these are in manufacturing, wholesale and retail trade, construction, hospitality and community services. Since 1968, employment in manufacturing and agriculture has declined but it has increased in community services, personal services, finance and other service industries. This pattern is in line with that of other industrialised countries and is expected to continue.

Part-time work has risen significantly in the last two decades, accounting for two-fifths of the total increase in the employed labour force.

Defence

Although Australia's relations with countries in its region remain sound, it accepts that it must be able, from its own resources, to defend itself and its direct interests.

Self-reliance is pursued within a framework of alliances and arrangements with countries of its region.

The defence task is made daunting by the country's size, vast coastline and relatively small population. To be feasible the task requires careful integration of intelligence and surveillance, maritime patrol and response and rapid mobile reaction ground-force capabilities.

The strategy of defence in depth relies on that integration.

Defence planning is based on a realistic assessment of the levels of force that could be brought against Australia if strategic circumstances should change. It requires the Australian Defence Force to be able to respond effectively to the lesser threats that could arise in the shorter term.

At the same time Australia sets out to create an environment in which the likelihood of either kind of threat is minimised.

To this end it has long supported the efforts of the ASEAN states, Papua New Guinea and the island states of the south-west Pacific to develop their economic and political resilience and strengthen their mutual cooperation in defence. It does so via a program of civil and military cooperation and assistance. At the same time it maintains its involvement in the Five Power Defence Arrangements with Malaysia, Singapore, New Zealand and Britain.

Of even longer standing has been Australia's cooperation with the United States and New Zealand in the ANZUS Alliance. Despite differences that have arisen in recent years between the US and New Zealand about visits by US warships to New Zealand, which have seriously affected their cooperation, the ANZUS Alliance itself remains, Australia-US defence cooperation is undiminished and Australia maintains close defence ties with New Zealand.

The ANZUS Treaty expresses Australia's continuing support for broader Western security interests and provides a basis for cooperation in the deterrence of global conflict and support for arms-control proposals.

Australia's total defence outlay is about a tenth of federal expenditure.

Air and ground military forces on exercise

The Navy, Army and Air Force retain individual identities but are trained and commanded as arms of one national Defence Force. The combined strength of the Defence Force, including reservists, is about 100 000.

The Royal Australian Navy (RAN) is modern. Its front-line fleet comprises three guided-missile destroyers, four guided-missile frigates, five destroyer escorts and six Oberon-class submarines. Eight frigates and six submarines (Kockums type 471) will have been added to it by about the turn of the century.

Thirteen Fremantle-class patrol boats perform surveillance and fisheries-protection tasks. Two others are used for fleet support and training, and three Attack-class patrol boats are also used for Reserve training.

The RAN also has two supply vessels, one training ship, an amphibious heavy-lift ship, six heavy landing craft, three oceanograph-hydrographic ships and three mine-counter-measure vessels. The Fleet Air Arm uses only two fixed-wing aircraft (electronic warfare HS748s) and 31 helicopters, including 16 Seahawk S-70B-2 anti-submarine and surveillance helicopters.

The Army is an all-volunteer force of regular and reserve components organised on a command system comprising:

- Land Command — units formed within a divisional structure of three brigades, with combat and logistic support units;
- Logistic Command — general-support logistic units and installations in Australia;
- Training Command — training units and installations throughout Australia.

There are seven military districts, the boundaries of each of which approximates a state or territory.

Soldiers at Canberra Army Memorial ceremony

The Royal Australian Air Force is organised on a command system comprising:

- Air Command — responsible for the command of operational units and conduct of their activities;
- Support Command — responsible for the training of personnel and supplying and maintaining equipment.

The flying establishment comprises training units and operational squadrons. Two operational squadrons are equipped with F111C strike/reconnaissance aircraft, two with McDonnell-Douglas F/A-18 tactical fighters, and two with Orion maritime reconnaissance aircraft. Two medium-range transport squadrons and a medium- and long-range special transport squadron are equipped with Hercules C130 and Boeing 707 aircraft. Two tactical transport squadrons have Caribou aircraft. A special transport squadron operates BAC-One-Eleven, Mystere 20 and HST 718s and is re-equipping with Falcon 900s.

Training aircraft include piston-engined CT4 air-trainers and PC9 prop-jets for pilot training, as well as HS-748s for navigation and air-electronics training. Lead-in fighter training is done in Aeromacchi jets.

Civilian officers play an important role in formulating policy for strategic planning, force development and analysis, conditions of service, and financial planning as well as the design, acquisition and maintenance of equipment, training, and research and development. They work closely with the Australian Defence Force Headquarters and officers of the individual services.

The secretary of the Department of Defence and the Chief of the Defence Force are responsible jointly for the general administration of the Defence Force.

The Chief of the Defence Force exercises command through the three service chiefs of staff and is principal military adviser to the Minister for Defence. The secretary is the principal civilian adviser to the minister and, in particular, advises on general policy and on the management of resources.

The Defence Science and Technology Organisation (DSTO) in the Department of Defence has 1100 scientists and engineers and a total staff of about 4400, conducting research, in response to the Defence organisation's requirements. These range from major equipment to meet the unique demands of the region, such as the Jindalee over-the-horizon radar to monitor the northern approaches, to maintaining or adapting equipment and solving operational problems or analysing requirements for optimum purchase or use of military equipment.

DSTO has an extensive scientific and technological base and undertakes joint research with tertiary-education institutions, allied defence scientists and industry. It earns part of its income from industry and has contributed to technological knowledge in such fields as materials and equipment life extension, infra-red imaging, signal processing, diamond-hard lens coating and a range of laser applications.

'Outrider' organisations of the Department of Defence include the Natural Disasters Organisation (civil defence), the Joint Intelligence Organisation and the Defence Signals Directorate.

Health

Health care in Australia relies largely on a meshing of private and public facilities: a predominantly private medical profession, private and public hospitals and private and public health financing. In recent years, the system has been diversifying to include community health centres (which often have salaried medical staff) and, increasingly, home care.

Most primary health care is provided by private practitioners, who charge their patients directly and set their own fees. Some is provided by the staff of health centres and public hospitals, who may also exercise their right to practise privately.

Patients receive hospital care in either private or public hospitals. The choice is theirs, although most rely heavily on the advice of their medical practitioners.

Medicare, the universal national health-insurance system, is funded in part by a special levy on income and in part by general taxation. It provides access to public-hospital services and benefits for out-of-hospital medical expenses, equal to 85 per cent of a specified fee. This gap (between fee and reimbursement) and the system provides that the gap will not exceed $20 for a single service provided the specified fee has been charged. Charges beyond the specified fee are the patient's responsibility. Similar benefits apply to optometrical services.

Under Medicare, public hospitals are funded by the Federal Government and state governments. All Australian residents and certain categories of visitors have access, without direct charge, to public-hospital accommodation and to inpatient and outpatient treatment by doctors appointed by the hospital concerned.

If a patient in a public hospital specifies treatment by a specific doctor (that is, not a hospital appointee), he or she is treated as a private patient and is charged for accommodation. The chosen doctor charges independently for services rendered (and the patient is reimbursed under Medicare, but only to the level of 75 per cent of the specified fee).

Private hospitals charge for their services and are funded from the revenue thus generated. Private insurance is available to cover most of their charges. Doctors treating patients in private hospitals charge them independently and

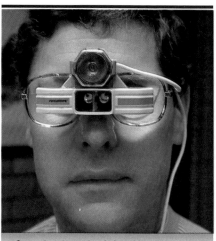

Surgeon's periscope views body cavities

the same benefits apply to such charges as in the public-hospital situation.

Private health-insurance organisations offer a range of benefits to cover hospital charges. They also offer benefits for ancillary services not covered by Medicare, such as dental, physiotherapy and chiropractic treatment. They are not permitted to offer medical-treatment cover for other than the 25 per cent gap for inpatient services.

Australia has more than 1000 hospitals — excluding psychiatric hospitals and nursing homes — most of them public. There are about six hospital beds per 1000 population.

Health-program grants are paid to organisations that provide health services approved by the Federal Government, such as family planning associations.

There are more than 30 000 practising doctors. Of the 20 universities, 10 have medical schools whose undergraduate courses last five or six years. Nearly half the practising doctors are general practitioners, about a third specialists in private practice and the rest salaried.

About 140 000 professionally registered nurses provide care in hospitals, nursing homes and home-nursing, occupational-health, and school and community health services. Authorisation to practise is controlled by governments.

Australia has more than 6000 dentists, most in private practice. Five universities provide five-year undergraduate courses. All states and territories operate school dental services, mainly to primary-school children.

Water supplies are fluoridated in most parts of Australia to prevent dental decay.

Public health services are provided by all levels of government. While they are the constitutional responsibility of state and local governments, the Federal Government is involved in setting national policies, which cover preventive medicine, communicable diseases, legal and illicit drugs, environmental hygiene, food nutrition, poisons, and pesticides. It also funds family planning, Aboriginal health and arbovirus disease control.

Organisations receive federal funds for national projects under the Community Health Program. The largest is the family medicine program of the Royal Australian College of General Practitioners, which provides vocational training for young doctors who intend to enter general practice.

Much of the identifiable health research is funded annually by the Federal Government on the advice of the National Health and Medical Research Council. Indirect federal medical-research funding includes grants to research institutes, universities and groups engaged in special investigations. Other funds are provided by state governments and non-government organisations.

The National Health and Medical Research Council is recognised as the authoritative body in Australia in matters of general health, public health and medical research.

Family-planning associations provide free teaching, counselling and related services. They receive specific funding from the Federal Government.

Aboriginals have the same entitlements to health services as all other Australians but many do not use them, partly for sociocultural reasons and partly because the general services are not equipped to deal with the severity of Aboriginal

Keeping fit and healthy aerobically

health problems. In an effort to overcome this problem the Federal Government funds Aboriginal-controlled health centres ranging from full-scale medical, dental and welfare units to smaller referral units with perhaps one doctor or nursing sister and some Aboriginal health workers. The Government also provides funds to states for such special health services as mobile medical teams or special treatment and/or preventive programs.

Health care for Aboriginals is primarily the responsibility of the state and territory health authorities.

The Federal Government has a national program of disease control aimed at all arboviral diseases.

The Royal Flying Doctor Service, begun half a century ago by the Reverend John Flynn, of the Presbyterian Church, serves people living in isolated places. In an emergency, a caller can be speaking to a doctor by radio within two or three minutes, 24 hours a day. There are 12 main bases, so few patients are more than two hours from medical help. The service includes regular clinic visits to all remote communities, visits by specialists and, in some areas, by dentists.

State education authorities use the Flying Doctor Service radio network for the 'School of the Air', which supplements the children's formal, state-run correspondence-course education. The service, registered as a charitable organisation, receives money from the Australian and state governments and from private donors.

The Red Cross Society is the official auxiliary of the medical services of the Australian Defence Forces. Apart from its relief activities, the society provides an almost universally used blood-transfusion service. Its cost is shared by the society with the federal, state and territory governments.

Drug education

Australia shares with many countries some of the problems and all of the concerns related to drug abuse.

The approach to the problem adopted in Australia relies, for its long-term effectiveness, on education. Providing education programs on drug abuse is principally the responsibility of the individual states and territories but their governments collaborate with the Federal Government to achieve a coordinated and cost-effective approach.

Two national campaigns — the National Campaign Against Drug Abuse and The Drug Offensive — are conducted on this issue. The former, involving direct federal funding and cost-sharing arrangements with state and territory governments, pursues general community education (including the use of the media), drug-education programs for parents and children, and training for professionals, including physicians, corrective-services personnel and teachers. The latter has had success in making the public aware of the extent and costs of drug abuse and of specific issues.

Per-capita consumption of total absolute alcohol rose by 48 per cent between 1963 and 1974 (from 6.6 litres to 9.8) but between 1978 and 1987 fell by 11 per cent to 8.7. Australia ranks about fifteenth in the world in alcohol consumption and is the tenth-largest consumer of beer. In recent years, low-alcohol beers have achieved significant market penetration.

Emphasis is being given now to making the community aware of the dangers of excessive drinking, and to making health professionals aware of the likelihood that much ill-health is related to alcohol misuse. The incidence of alcohol-related deaths has been falling in recent years.

Continuing efforts by health authorities seem to be reducing the incidence of smoking.

History

In the second century AD the Greek geographer Ptolemy sketched a map of the known coasts of Asia, showing the Indian Ocean as a vast lake and a big unknown land, called Terra Incognita, to its south. European merchant ships, visiting Asia, found it there 1500 years later.

In 1606, Luis Vaez de Torres sailed through the strait (since named after him) which separates Australia and Papua New Guinea. Months later Willem Janszoon sailed into the Gulf of Carpentaria and, 17 years later, Jan Carstensz charted and named the main features of the western coast of Cape York. His writing on the terrain lacked enthusiasm.

By that time other Dutch navigators had reached parts of the northern and western coast. Dirck Hartog examined the west coast near Shark Bay in 1616. Abel Tasman visited and named Van Diemen's Land, now Tasmania, in 1642 and, two years later, charted roughly the coast from Cape York to the Ashburton River, Western Australia. The Dutch called the continent New Holland.

The first English visitor was William Dampier, a buccaneer, who landed near King Sound, on the north-west coast, in 1688. He came back 10 years later in the Royal Navy ship Roebuck to continue exploring, but the first to see the east coast was the British Royal Navy's Captain James Cook, in 1770. Having visited Tahiti to make astronomical observations he sailed south-west in Endeavour, circumnavigated New Zealand and headed west. He sighted land near Cape Everard, in the south-east corner of Australia. He turned north, charting the coastline as he went, and landed at Botany Bay, which he named for the variety of plant life there.

Cook continued north nearly 3000km until his ship struck a coral reef near Cooktown, Queensland. After two months' repair work he sailed north and, after passing through Torres Strait, landed on an island 3km off Cape York. Naming it Possession Island, he raised the British flag and took formal possession of the eastern part of the continent.

Cook's account of his discovery aroused much interest in England but Britain did not try to colonise Australia until its American colonies achieved independence. Britain then needed new places where it could transport its criminals.

Eleven ships commanded by Captain Arthur Phillip left England in May 1787 and reached Botany Bay on January 18, 1788. They left eight days later because of the bay's poor soils and openness, and settled instead at Port Jackson, a few kilometres north. The ships landed 1373 people, including 732 convicts. The settlement became Sydney.

On January 26, 1788, Phillip took formal possession of the whole eastern part of the continent, including Tasmania.

For a few years the colonists depended for food almost entirely on imported supplies but better soils were found at nearby Parramatta and they became more self-sufficient. Exploratory coastal voyages were made, the most important that of Captain Matthew Flinders who, in 1802–03, circumnavigated the continent.

The Blue Mountains, part of the Great Dividing Range extending almost unbroken down the east coast of Australia, prevented westward expansion of the settlement until 1813, when a way was found over them by Gregory Blaxland, William Wentworth and William Lawson. Then exploration went ahead although, for many years, only a few expeditions went west.

Allan Cunningham, a botanist, discovered the rich Darling Downs of southern Queensland, and John Oxley, a surveyor, found the Brisbane River. Hamilton Hume, the son of an agriculturist, and William Hovell, a trader-settler, went south and reached the Southern Ocean, west of Melbourne's present site.

Captain Charles Sturt, who arrived in 1827, traced the Lachlan River and others flowing inland from the coastal mountains, reaching the Darling in 1829, and found that many other known rivers were its tributaries. Major Thomas Mitchell, the surveyor-general, went overland to Cape Northumberland in south-eastern South Australia in 1836 and returned through Victoria as far east as Port Phillip Bay.

Settlements were established at Hobart in 1803; on the Brisbane River in 1824; and on the Swan River in 1829. Melbourne was established on Port Phillip Bay in 1835, and Adelaide in 1836. These settlements became the capital cities of five states.

Early governors were able to grant land free to anyone — emancipated convicts,

View of Sydney Cove, an aquatint from a painting by John Eyre c.1771–1812. National Library of Australia.

free settlers, marines and officers of the garrison — willing to employ, feed and clothe convicts. The free population increased rapidly, as did the colonies' herds, and settlement spread to the western plains. The settlers needed a staple trading industry, as the early whaling, sealing and subsistence agriculture were to be short-lived solutions. In the late 1700s Captain John Macarthur and others began experiments in breeding fine-wool sheep using Spanish merinos from Cape Province, South Africa, and others from the royal flocks at Kew, England. These experiments at Camden, near Sydney, laid the foundations of the country's economic development. The merino was transformed gradually into a superior woolgrowing animal. Accustomed to the dry Spanish plains, merinos adapted well to the climate. The wool industry flourished and the population grew from 34 000 in 1820 to 405 000 in 1850.

Public agitation forced an end to convict transportation to the mainland in 1840 and to Tasmania 13 years later. By then, 100 000 of them had arrived. Western Australia, which had not received convicts previously but was very short of labour, elected to receive quotas between 1850 and 1868.

Gold was discovered in 1851 at Bathurst, New South Wales, then at Ballarat and Bendigo, Victoria, and people rushed to these gold strikes from many parts of the world. As the richest of the alluvial goldfields were worked out and companies began to mine gold-bearing reefs, many individual miners took up farming.

The colonies were widely separated and far from the motherland, and governing them was administratively impracticable. Self-government became an objective and, in 1823, New South Wales was granted the first constitutional

charter by a British law authorising creation of a council with limited legislative power. Two years later Tasmania, which had been tied to NSW, formed a similar council. Western Australia and South Australia, politically distinct from New South Wales since settlement, formed such councils in 1838 and 1842. In 1842 Britain extended the New South Wales Legislative Council's powers and allowed two-thirds of its membership to be elected on a restricted franchise. Queensland (the Moreton Bay District of New South Wales) and Victoria continued to be represented in the Legislative Council of New South Wales.

The British Government's Australian Colonies Government Act 1850 empowered the colonies to establish legislatures, determine the franchise and frame constitutions. In 1851, Victoria gained its legislature under the Act.

New South Wales was the first to draft a new constitution, in 1855. All other colonies except Western Australia became self-governing in 1859. Western Australia's decision to become a penal colony in 1850 delayed responsible government until 1890.

The need to protect or promote common interests led to a series of intercolonial conferences of premiers held at irregular intervals from 1863.

A draft federal constitution was drawn up in 1891 at a convention sponsored by the Premier of New South Wales, Sir Henry Parkes. A further convention in 1897-98 turned it into the Australian Constitution. The Commonwealth of Australia — a federation of the six former colonies as states — came into being on January 1, 1901.

Primary industry

Australia, whose first European settlers in Australia had to import virtually all their food for many years after they arrived, has become one of the world's major exporters of agricultural products. It is the world's largest producer of wool and exports large quantities of cereals, dairy produce, meat, sugar and fruit.

Its 170 000-plus agricultural and pastoral properties cover about two-thirds of its land area. More than nine-tenths of the land is used mainly for light grazing. The rest is cultivated for agriculture and intensive grazing.

Lack of water is the main factor limiting agricultural production. Only about a fifth of the continent, mainly in the northern and eastern coasts and in Tasmania, receives an annual rainfall of 600 mm or more. Other limiting factors are fragile and relatively infertile, nutrient-deficient soils and difficult terrain.

Despite such limitations, rural output has increased substantially since the early 1950s, mainly because of advances in agricultural technology and science, a big increase in farm mechanisation and expanding markets for several major products.

Today, the agricultural sector accounts for less than a twentieth of gross domestic product but still accounts for about a third of export income.

Australia has about a sixth of the world's sheep and produces a third of the world's wool. Wool production has reached about 1000 million kilograms, coming from the predominant merino breed.

The wool-growing industry is among Australia's rural export leaders. Wool export earnings commonly eclipse all others, running at about $6000 million a year. Most of Australia's wool is exported, mainly to Japan, Western Europe, the Soviet Union and China, and provides nearly three-quarters of the world's apparel-wool exports.

Second only to New Zealand in the export of sheep meat, Australia nonetheless consumes about two-thirds of its own production. It leads the world in the export of live sheep for slaughter at

Golden wheat ready for harvest

destination. In the late 1980s it was selling seven million head a year to the Middle East, and North African markets were beginning to develop.

The proportions are reversed for beef and veal, even though domestic consumption of these meats averages about 40kg per capita and production runs at 1.3 million to 2 million tonnes a year. Nearly two-thirds of it is exported. The United States is by far Australia's largest overseas customer, followed by Japan.

Almost all of Australia's substantial production of pig and poultry meat is sold on the domestic market.

The dairy industry is mainly in the south-eastern coastal region of the mainland and in northern Tasmania, where rainfall is ample and reliable. Whole-milk production is more than 6000 million litres, valued at more than $1600 million. About a quarter is sold domestically as whole milk (including flavoured and Ultra High Temperature) and the rest is used in butter, cheese,

Colourful display of vegetables grown on Australian farms

condensed milk products, milk powder, casein and cream. About half these products are exported.

Egg production is around 200 million dozen a year. Very few are exported.

Australia produces between 25 000 and 30 000 tonnes of honey a year and exports nearly half.

Wheat production averages about 15 million tonnes a year. Most of it is exported, making Australia the world's fourth-largest wheat exporter.

The largest export markets are Iran, Iraq, Egypt, China and Japan. Important regular markets include the Middle East, South-East Asia and the Pacific region. The domestic requirement, including that for seed and feed, is about three million tonnes a year.

Barley, oats, sorghum, maize and triticale are the main coarse-grain crops, and small crops of rye and millet are grown. Production varies considerably from year to year according to seasonal and market conditions. Barley is grown for stock feed and for malt. The other coarse grains are used mainly for compounding into stock feed.

Annual rice production has varied from 519 000 tonnes from the drought-affected 1982–83 crop to a record 864 000 tonnes in 1984–85. Nearly all is grown in southern NSW and the rest in northern Queensland. A large proportion of the crop is exported, mainly to Papua New Guinea, Hong Kong, the Pacific islands and the Middle East.

Oilseed production has grown about fivefold since the early 1970s. NSW and Queensland produce nearly all of it (mostly cottonseed and sunflower), satisfying more than half the country's vegetable-oil requirements.

Grain-legume production has increased sevenfold and more since the early 1980s. About half is exported, mainly to the European Community, India and Japan. Lupins and field peas are predominant and lupin exports to the EC for animal- feed production are the largest single item.

Cotton is grown in north-western NSW and southern and central Queensland, mostly on irrigated plantations. In recent times production has grown from being barely adequate for local spinners' needs to the point where nearly all of it is exported. The major markets are Japan, Taiwan Province, Republic of Korea and Yugoslavia.

All Australia's sugar is produced in the coastal north-eastern regions of Queensland and northern NSW. Important milling by-products include bagasse (fibre), molasses, ash and filter mud. The yield is usually about three million tonnes of raw sugar, four-fifths of which is exported. Japan is the main export market and other major customers are Canada, Republic of Korea, Malaysia, China and Singapore.

Australia's wide climatic variations allow the cultivation of many types of tropical and temperate fruit. The most important are grapes, citrus, apples, bananas, pears, peaches and pineapples.

Commercially, apples are one of the most important fruits grown. Exports of fresh apples range from 25 000 to 30 000 tonnes a year and the other 90 per cent are consumed domestically. Victoria produces four-fifths of the country's pears; annual exports of fresh pears (about a quarter of the crop) have averaged 37 000 tonnes in recent years.

More than three-quarters of Australian citrus is grown in the irrigated inland areas of NSW, Victoria and South Australia. Production has averaged about 600 000 tonnes in recent years and fresh exports about a tenth of that.

Northern NSW and Queensland are the main banana-producing areas. Australia's banana production has averaged 145 000 tonnes in recent years. Pineapple production, almost entirely in Queensland, has averaged 135 000 tonnes.

Canning of apricots, peaches and pears, four-fifths of which is done in Victoria, averages about 90 000 tonnes. More than half is exported.

Dried-vine-fruit production runs at about 84 000 tonnes, most of which is exported. The main buyers are the Federal Republic of Germany, Canada, New Zealand, Britain and Japan.

Australia's average annual wine output is about 400 million litres, most of it consumed domestically. Exports are increasing as its reputation spreads and now constitute about a tenth of production. By volume, Sweden is the main buyer, followed by the United Kingdom, New Zealand, Japan and Denmark. More than half Australia's wine is produced in South Australia.

The wide range of climates and soils in Australia enables most types of vegetables to be grown. Potatoes are most widely cultivated, followed by peas, tomatoes, pumpkins and beans. About a million tonnes of potatoes are grown each year.

Australia's forests are managed for timber production, water catchment, flora and fauna protection and public recreation.

Key forestry objectives are the efficient and sustainable development of resources and the promotion of environmentally sensitive management practices — a sound balance of resource use, preservation, conservation and development.

The extensive forests in the higher rainfall zones of eastern and south-west Australia are highly productive. With plantations of exotic and native species, many of these forests are the resource base for major industries.

Native forests cover nearly 41 million ha, three-quarters of which are dominated by eucalypts. Plantations for timber production total about a million ha. A further 65 million ha are classified as eucalypt woodland, mainly tropical, sub-tropical and semi-arid. Native forests are predominantly hardwoods but include some conifers.

The turnover of the forest products industry runs at more than $7000 million a year.

Commercial fish production has been fairly stable in recent years. The most important commercial fish are tuna and salmon for canning, and table fish such as mullet, shark, whiting, snapper and gemfish. Exports average about $600 million a year.

Prawns and rock lobsters are Australia's most valuable fishing resources and the main seafood export earners (17 000 and 15 000 tonnes a year respectively). Almost all abalone (annual catch about 6600 tonnes) is exported. The scallop catch is about 9000 tonnes.

R esources and energy

When the extent of Australia's arid area — most of the interior — and remote and rugged regions became known in the 1800s, settlers living in the coastal colonies could have been forgiven for despairing of its long-term future.

Many parts of what the colonists saw as barren, useless land have been yielding wealth beyond anything they could have imagined, as minerals and energy resources no-one in the world of those days had heard of.

One example was bauxite, a mineral discovered lying on and in the ground by the thousand million tonnes. Australia is now the world's largest bauxite (from which comes alumina) and alumina producer, the largest alumina exporter and a major exporter of bauxite, and still has vast reserves.

Australia has become one of the world's major producers of minerals and metals. It has major deposits of black and brown coal, mineral sands, gold, lead, zinc, iron, copper, nickel, manganese, uranium and diamonds.

A major producer and exporter of energy resources and one of only five net energy exporters in the OECD, Australia is the world's largest exporter of coal and a major exporter of uranium, and exports significant quantities of light crude oil (although it imports heavy crude). It exports increasingly large quantities of liquefied natural gas.

Crude oil and natural gas
Substantial oil and gas discoveries have been made in Australia in the last three decades. There is good potential for more, as many sedimentary basins have been explored only lightly. Discoveries in recent years in the Timor Sea and off Western Australia underscore this potential and tests of new exploration concepts are encouraging.

Australian demand for petroleum products is satisfied mainly by domestic refining capacity, using both domestic and imported crudes. Domestic refining capacity is modern and second only to Singapore's in the South-East Asian region.

Miners drill at Mt Isa silver-lead-zinc mine

Australia exports refined petroleum products to meet regional requirements, particularly in the South Pacific.

Total proved and probable reserves of Australian crude oil and condensate exceed 1600 million barrels.

Coal

The world's largest exporter and seventh-largest producer of black coal, Australia has estimated reserves of more than 500 000 million tonnes, about two-thirds of which is considered recoverable. About a tenth of it comes under the heading of demonstrated, economically recoverable resources. Almost all of it is in NSW and Queensland.

About half Australia's coal exports in recent years have gone to Japan but sales to other Asian countries and Europe are increasing.

Uranium

Australia's reasonably assured uranium resources represent nearly a third of the Western world's uranium resources. The major deposits are in the Northern Territory, South Australia and Western Australia.

Uranium mining and export are permitted from only the Ranger and Nabarlek mines in the Northern Territory and the Olympic Dam mine in South Australia and are subject to stringent safeguard requirements. Nabarlek finished processing its high-grade ore in 1988. Ranger produces about 3000 tonnes of uranium oxide a year, but could double production. The Olympic Dam copper-uranium-gold project began commercial production of uranium concentrates in 1988 at about 1500 tonnes a year of uranium oxide.

Iron ore mining at Pilbara region, Western Australia, using a giant mechanical shovel

Iron ore

The world's second-largest exporter of iron ore, Australia produces about 100 million tonnes a year and has demonstrated economic resources of more than 15 000 million tonnes of high-grade ore. Western Australia, which has mines that are among the world's largest, produces most.

Bauxite/alumina/aluminium

The largest producer in the world of both bauxite and alumina, Australia is also the third-largest producer of aluminium and exports three-quarters of its output. Australia also exports three-quarters of its alumina, accounting for about half the world's alumina trade.

Lead and zinc

Australia has substantial resources of lead and zinc and is one of the world's major producers and exporters. Lead and zinc are mined mainly in NSW, Queensland, Tasmania and Western Australia.

Lead refinery-smelters operate in Queensland, NSW and South Australia. The Port Pirie (South Australia) smelter is the largest in the world. One of the world's major zinc refineries is at Risdon, Tasmania.

Copper

Demonstrated economic resources of copper in Australia are large, several major deposits having been discovered in the 1980s. It is mined in all states except Victoria and refineries operate in Queensland, NSW and South Australia. More than half the country's output of refined copper — about 250 000 tonnes — is exported.

Bauxite arrives by train at refinery at Weipa

Nickel

Australia ranks third in world mine output of nickel, and exports nearly all of it. In Western Australia, where economic resources of nickel sulphide ore are large, the ore is processed to nickel matte and metal for export. Nickel laterite ore mined in Queensland is processed into nickel oxide but is nearing exhaustion.

Gold

There has been a significant upsurge in gold exploration since the early 1980s, placing Australia third among the western world's producers and its gold in third position also among Australia's export-income earners.

There are substantial demonstrated economic resources and most is produced in Western Australia and Queensland. The development of technology permitting low-cost recovery of low-grade ore and tailings abandoned years ago as uneconomic has stimulated an increase in production.

Mineral sands

Australia is the leading producer of rutile, zircon, monazite and alluvial ilmenite. All of these minerals have high-technology applications in aerospace work, advanced ceramics, lasers and fibre optics. The industry has been developing projects for further processing — producing, for example, titanium dioxide pigment, high-purity zirconia and rare earths.

Other minerals

The manganese mine on Groote Eylandt, in the Northern Territory, is one of the world's largest mines and Australia is one of only three major world exporters of the mineral. Ore and refined forms (ferro-alloys and electrolytic manganese dioxide) are also produced. Tin ore is another mineral produced, most of it exported to Malaysia for refining.

Australia is also the world's largest producer by volume of diamonds and the world's leading producer of sapphires and opals.

Electricity

Each state has its own pattern of electric power development. Electricity is generated mainly by burning coal; natural gas and hydro-electric power are other sources of electricity.

While hydro-electric energy accounts for about a ninth of all electricity generated in Australia, the Snowy Mountains hydro-electric scheme in south-east Australia remains one of the country's greatest engineering undertakings and one of the world's larger irrigation and power projects. The scheme, which diverts water inland from coastal watersheds, has seven power stations, a pumping station, 16 large and many smaller dams, 145km of tunnels and 80km of aqueducts, and took 25 years to build. Its generating capacity is 3740 megawatts.

Energy policy

Energy policy in Australia is formulated to be consistent with major economic, industrial and social objectives and its key goals are:
- security of overall energy supplies;
- development of the energy exports sector; and
- efficiency in the domestic energy sector.

The policy is intended to provide the right framework to ensure that Australia has access to the appropriate mix of energy supplies to meet its changing needs.

The nation is committed to continued research into and development of renewable energy, energy conservation, efficient energy use and alternative fuels. It maintains a major geological and geophysical research and investigation program.

Australia is an active member of the International Energy Agency and other international organisations.

Domestically, there is considerable consultation on energy matters. The main advisory and consultative bodies are: Australian Minerals and Energy Council, National Energy Consultative Council, National Energy Research, Development and Demonstration Council and the National Oil Supplies Advisory Committee.

M anufacturing industry

Australia is a dynamic economy, enjoying political stability, generous natural resources, a skilled workforce, steady population growth and substantial domestic and foreign capital investment.

For a number of years the Australian economy has been undergoing a major restructuring, the goal of which has been the greater flexibility and efficiency needed for Australian industry to compete successfully in global markets.

The country has a broad industrial base, able to produce manufactured goods ranging from fashion garments to food, complex electronic devices to household appliances, base metals to precision instruments, through to oil refining and plastics.

Although it has a relatively small domestic market, it has the advantage of being geographically part of the Asia-Pacific region, which is developing into a major centre of economic activity.

A high level of capital investment has been a significant factor in the growth of Australian manufacturing. Overseas capital has been important to expansion, particularly in the motor-vehicle, chemical and oil-refining industries, but most funds have been generated domestically.

Many Australian companies manufacture under licence from overseas, but there has been much domestic innovation — mainly in manufacturing — which has resulted in overseas licensing of many Australian-devised products and processes.

Manufactures represent more than a quarter of Australia's total exports.

The tertiary or service sector is the largest segment of the Australian economy and has been growing in importance relative to the other major sectors. Services employ about three-quarters of the workforce and contribute about two-thirds of the gross domestic product.

The retail and wholesale trades are the largest employers, followed by community services and construction. Other major employers are transport, communication, financial and business services, energy and water reticulation, entertainment, recreation and personal

Retail display of designer clothing

services, public administration and defence. The sector's share of the gross domestic product is around 60 per cent.

Small business, numerically about 96 per cent of private-sector, non-agricultural enterprises, is dynamic and healthy in Australia and it employs nearly half the non-farm workforce.

About 80 companies, employing about 12 000 people, are involved in the Australian aerospace industry. Most of the industry's $900 million turnover is generated by 10 manufacturers, which design, manufacture and assemble a range of air platforms and components and undertake major repair and overhaul of engines, airframes and avionics. Exports represent about a third of the industry's turnover.

The chemicals and plastics industries use local and imported raw materials to produce a wide range of intermediate and final products. Major groupings in the industries include petrochemicals, fertilisers, plastics, pharmaceuticals, agricultural chemicals, soaps and detergents.

Making boots for export

Australia manufactures chemical fertilisers, plastics, synthetic rubber, agricultural and veterinary chemicals, explosives, paint, dyes, textile fibres, adhesives, pharmaceuticals, detergents and solvents. The major plastics are polyethylene (high and low density) polyvinyl chloride, amino resins (urea and melamines), alkyd resins, polystyrene and its copolymers, polypropylene and polyurethane.

There are about 1300 plastics-processing establishments producing a wide range of plastic products such as packaging materials, automotive components, pipes and fittings, house-hold wares and building materials.

Imported drugs and materials are combined with local products to produce patent medicines, ethical preparations and biological substances such as vaccines. Processing conforms with international technology.

The Australian electrical industry meets a substantial part of the local demand for domestic and industrial electrical products, particularly household appliances. Australia produces a wide range of electric motors, control gear, switch gear and electric wire and cables. The transformer industry supplies almost all the needs of the Australian market.

The Australian electronics and information-based industries supply most of the local market for telecommunications equipment and have considerable strengths in software development and the design and production of advanced medical, scientific and defence equipment and specialised electronic components, small computers and terminals.

Australia's engineering industries produce a wide range of hand and machine tools, metalworking machinery and materials-handling equipment. Light-engineering industries make such varied products as roller bearings, die castings, forgings, many types of measuring and recording instruments, valves and control equipment, television antennas, pumping, ventilating and heating equipment, fasteners such as nails, nuts, bolts and rivets and many other metal products.

Complex heavy-duty and automatic machines of many types and sizes are made, including railway rolling stock, diesel-electric locomotives, pumps, passenger and commercial motor vehicles, and earthmoving and excavating equipment, agricultural equipment and tractors.

There is extensive construction of small to medium-sized ships, including small trading vessels and specialised vessels such as tugs, dredges, barges, fishing boats, passenger ferries and oil-rig service boats.

Australia is a major and efficient producer of a diverse range of agricultural products of the highest standard, much sought after by food manufacturers worldwide.

Car bodies are assembled at motor vehicle manufacturing plant

The Australian food-processing industry is the largest manufacturing sector, supplying almost the entire domestic market, and exporting goods worth more than $1000 million a year.

The Australian food-processing industry comprises a number of major international corporations using Australia as a base for supplying the Asia-Pacific market.

There is massive potential for the processing in Australia of its agricultural products and there is general acceptance that the industry will develop into a major supplier of such products to the growing international market.

The industry is innovative and a world leader in important aspects of food technology.

Australia's abundant mineral resources and competitive energy prices contribute to the expansion of further processing of minerals and metals. In recent years, mineral-sands processing and aluminium production have been prominent in this expansion and there have been large increases in research and development in minerals-processing technology. Important new resource bodies have been found in the same period.

A long-established domestic industry supplies most of Australia's manufactured tobacco — virtually all cigarettes, a quarter of cigars, cigarillos and cheroots and more than half the other products.

The motor-vehicle industry comprises five manufacturers — General Motors Holden's Automotive, Ford Australia, Toyota Motor Corporation of Australia, Mitsubishi Motors Australia and Nissan Australia — which supply four-fifths of Australian demand (more than 300 000 passenger vehicles a year) and export vehicles and components worth more than $600 million a year.

Oil refining is of great significance to the Australian economy. Most manufacturing industries and commerce depend on its products and refineries are located in each mainland state, some with associated petrochemical complexes.

The main products from Australian oil refineries are motor spirit, automotive distillate, fuel oil (including bunkers), liquefied petroleum gas, aviation turbine fuel and industrial diesel fuel.

Thirty-four establishments manufacture pulp, paper or paperboard in Australia and supply about three-quarters of domestic requirements.

The textile and clothing industries process natural and synthetic fibres to produce many apparel and textile goods. Australia produces most of its natural fibres. The textiles industry produces yarns, fabrics and most finished textile products, including wool, cotton, synthetic fibres and mixtures. Finished textile fabrics produced in Australia include carpets, domestic textiles (such as bed linen and curtains) and industrial textiles.

Most of the footwear industry is in Melbourne and Sydney. Australian manufacturers produce a wide range of footwear using a variety of materials, including leather, textiles and plastics, and account for half the domestic market.

Education

Each state and territory of Australia has its own primary and secondary education system. Standards, however, are high and reasonably uniform.

Within each state and territory system there are two main types of school — government and non-government. In the former, attended by about two-thirds of children, tuition is free. Of the latter, run mostly by religious bodies, about three-quarters are Catholic. Most non-government schools charge fees.

Throughout Australia, schooling is compulsory between the ages of six and 15 years (16 in Tasmania). However, most children begin school earlier than the law requires, generally in pre-schools run by the organisations that administer the mainstream schools.

Primary schooling lasts six to seven years and the curriculum is similar across the nation. Studies begin with basic language and mathematics and the fundamentals of inquiry, and social, health and creative skills are taught. Before reaching secondary level, children are learning English, mathematics, elementary science, social studies, music, art, craft and physical education. Optional subjects such as religion, languages and music are common.

Secondary schooling begins at year seven or eight and goes typically to year 12. More advanced levels of the same subjects are taught, plus technical and commercial ones. The typical secondary school is the co-educational comprehensive or multi-purpose high school, offering a wide range of subjects. Some states have separate high schools and colleges specialising in technical, agricultural, commercial and other fields. Their curriculums include general academic subjects and practical training.

Major examinations, or other formal assessments occur after three or four years of high school and at this point most students are old enough to leave the system. Another two years' study is available, however, and many keep going to the end — year 12. In most parts of Australia, certificates are issued at each of these levels, called commonly the School Certificate (at or about year 10) and the Higher School Certificate (year 12). The latter is normally required for university or higher-education college entry.

Primary school learning takes in many skills

The entire system is matched by correspondence courses for pupils prevented by illness, disability or residential isolation from attending schools. There are also "schools of the air", which use existing two-way radio networks to provide "classroom" experience to students in very isolated places.

Transport to most schools is either free or at reduced rates. In some states, children living too far from a secondary school to travel daily may live in hostels funded or subsidised by the government.

Although most Aboriginal and Torres Strait Islander students use the general school system, special programs exist to cater for the special qualities of their cultural heritage. Within these programs, Aboriginal teaching assistants, special advisers and resource teachers are employed and special curriculums, including bilingual programs, are developed.

Special programs exist also to help Aboriginal students to continue into higher education. They provide for living allowances, extra student places and other forms of support.

Special educational services are provided to integrate into classrooms children with disabilities attending special and mainstream schools. They are designed to accommodate the special needs of children with intellectual, physical, sensory, emotional, social or learning disabilities.

A nationwide program exists in schools designed to increase students' sensitivity to the Australian population's many different cultural backgrounds and to help ethnic communities maintain their languages and cultures.

Pre-school (kindergarten) children play in sandpit

Students from non-English-speaking backgrounds are helped to develop competence in English, to enhance their equality of opportunity in education and participation in society. Educational materials developed under federal initiatives are made available to schools to meet the language needs of these children.

State departments responsible for various aspects of education provide English-language classes, where necessary, for immigrants. Technical and evening colleges also offer literacy and secondary-level courses for adults preparing for matriculation and other public examinations.

The Federal Government provides financial help for students, including postgraduate awards, tertiary-education assistance, and secondary allowances and assistance schemes for Aboriginals. It also helps children who must live away from home or study by correspondence, and adult students returning to school to complete secondary education. Some allowances are subject to a means test on family income.

Pre-school and primary teachers, who usually teach the whole school curriculum, must complete three years of training in a college of advanced education.

Secondary teachers usually complete a degree course and professional training, acquiring a diploma of education or similar certificate. There is a trend toward integration from the outset of the professional and the degree studies. Specialist teachers (physical education, music, art) train for three to four years, either wholly in a teacher-training

institution or partly at another specialised institution.

Annual federal-government education expenditure at present exceeds $6000 million and has grown in recent years at about 10 per cent a year in dollar terms.

Post-secondary education in Australia occurs in universities, colleges of advanced education (CAEs) and colleges of technical and further education (TAFEs).

Although both universities and CAEs offered higher education (degree courses etc) before 1989, they had differing emphases. Both offered courses and undertook research in a range of academic and professional disciplines but the work in CAEs had a greater emphasis on vocation and CAE research programs were mainly in applied science and technology.

From 1989 the Federal Government removed formal distinctions between the two, expecting that mergers would reduce the total number of institutions eventually from 72 to about 35.

Although the states and territories are responsible for all education, the Federal Government provides most funding for higher education. In 1989, it set up a system under which both undergraduate and postgraduate students must make a financial contribution toward the cost of their study.

There are a few privately funded higher-education institutions, imcluding the Bond University of Technology, which took its first fee-paying students in 1989, three teachers' colleges and others, including theological colleges.

In the technical-education field, too, there are a few private colleges, but most of Australia's approximately one million

TAFE students attend its 215 state-administered colleges, undertaking pre-vocational, vocational, educational and recreational studies at levels ranging up to the para-professional. The vast majority study part-time.

TAFE colleges cover all major skills in a wide range of industrial, commercial, artistic and domestic occupations. They offer apprentices', trade, post-trade and technicians' courses, as well as commercial and general courses to certificate and diploma level.

The Federal Government is encouraging the entire secondary and post-secondary education sector to improve credit transfer between its parts.

Tertiary education is through universities and colleges of technical and further education

It is giving priority also to increasing the involvement of industry in education.

Adult education (also called continuing education) includes vocational and non-vocational courses. TAFE colleges provide both and most universities offer non-degree continuing-education programs. Some states fund councils or boards responsible for continuing education and, because of the growing demand for such education, voluntary bodies have become significant tuition providers.

Students and specialists are helped to study in Australia under international plans and scholarships; others study privately at Australian institutions. Tens of thousands of foreign students study in Australia each year at universities, colleges, secondary schools and private institutions.

The Australian National Commission for United Nations Educational, Scientific and Cultural Organisation (UNESCO) advises the Federal Government on Australia's participation in its programs, and supports its objectives. Its national committee has a network of advisory groups specialising in education, natural sciences, social sciences, culture and communication, and is responsible for a wide program of activities, including organising national and regional seminars.

Areas of university research and development include the humanities; the social, physical, biological, earth and applied sciences; engineering, agriculture, astronomy and medicine.

As a member of the OECD, Australia is able to exchange information about education and training with the 23 other industrialised member countries.

The legal system

Australia's system of law was inherited from, and resembles closely, the British system. Several important differences exist, however, mainly because Australia has a written constitution and a federal form of government.

It is administered in two "streams" — the statute law (including the "criminal code"), enacted by legislatures, and the common law, developed by the courts — and both evolve by interpretation in the courts, which often consider precedents set in earlier decisions.

The laws exist to protect and govern the community but of great importance under Australian law are the rights of the individual.

Lesser criminal matters are heard by magistrates or justices of the peace, who have power to convict and impose penalties.

Courts are usually open to the public but may be closed — to protect national security, for example, or the interests of young persons.

Juries, usually of 12 people in serious criminal cases and fewer in civil actions, are chosen randomly from the adult population and must possess certain qualities, such as having no criminal record. They decide questions of fact only, although in some civil jurisdictions they also assess damages. Judges decide questions of law only.

Only judges and magistrates (and sometimes justices of the peace) impose sentences. Although maximum criminal penalties, and often minimums, are specified, considerable discretion may be used to take account of specific circumstances.

Serious crime usually results in imprisonment or fines, or both. Capital punishment has not been practised in Australia for more than 20 years and has been generally abolished.

Australian statute law is created by parliaments, state and federal, and legislative assembles in the two main territories. Commonly these laws either embody or make provision for subsidiary legislation, called regulations or rules, which have the same authority, to be made by authorised individuals.

The common law is reasonably uniform in its basis but, in practice, significant differences exist because of laws enacted by state and territorial parliaments, none of which is subordinate to another.

Conditions of entry to the Australian legal profession are governed by federal, state and territory laws and rules. Requirements vary but, generally, at least five years' study and, thereafter, experience, is usual.

Judges, magistrates and others who preside over courts are government-appointed and those of the superior courts are chosen from the legal profession's ranks. Judges have security of tenure until their (fixed) retiring age and are free, by convention, from political interference.

Each of the states and territories has its own court system, and a federal system exists to deal with matters over which the national parliament has jurisdiction. Still, while the two levels are independent of one another, they are interdependent to an extent, partly because of the need for a measure of uniformity of law and order at the time of federation and partly because of legal and administrative convenience.

Under the Constitution, the judicial power of the Federal Government is vested in the High Court of Australia and any other courts the Federal Government creates. Two such are the Federal Court and the Family Court, which deal with specialised areas of federal law.

The High Court is at the apex and may deal with federal and state matters. It has original jurisdiction in important areas, including interpreting the Constitution and determining legal disputes between the Federal Government and state governments, litigation between state governments and claims between citizens from different states. It is the final court of appeal in Australia from both federal and state courts. The Chief Justice and six other justices preside over it.

The Federal Court, one of the specialised courts, deals with federal law in such areas as copyright, industrial law, trade practices, bankruptcy and administrative law, and appeals from cases decided by territory supreme courts and from other courts and tribunals administering federal laws.

The other specialised federal court, the Family Court, deals as far as the Constitution permits with divorce, custody of children and maintenance and associated property disputes. It is less formal than other courts.

All states and territories have supreme courts and magistrates' courts and several have intermediate ones called district or county courts. They are concerned mainly with state laws but have delegated power to deal with some federal matters, including those involving taxation and most federal criminal offences.

The supreme courts in each perform much the same roles at a state level as the High Court does federally. The district or county courts in most states are presided over by judges and determine most serious criminal matters as well as civil litigation up to certain monetary limits.

The magistrates' courts are presided over by magistrates and deal summarily (without a jury) with most ordinary offences — traffic infringements, minor assaults, street offences and the like — and preliminary hearings to decide whether prima-facie grounds exist in more serious cases for trial before a judge and jury. They also deal with lesser civil litigation for such things as debt recovery.

The Australian Capital Territory and the external territories of Norfolk Island, Christmas Island and the Cocos (Keeling) Islands have court systems similar to those of the states.

At both federal and state levels there exists the office of ombudsman, the occupants of which deal with a wide range of citizens' complaints against government administration.

There has been increasing emphasis in Australia for the last two decades on the protection of human rights and the elimination of inequalities in society. In 1973 Australia ratified the International Labour Organisation Convention on Discrimination in Employment and Occupation, and national and state committees were formed to investigate complaints of breaches of it. Since then anti-discrimination and other human-rights legislation has been enacted by the Federal Government and the governments of most states. Regulatory agencies have been set up to pursue complaints about breaches of such legislation.

The federal Human Rights and Equal Opportunities Commission, set up in 1986, can review legislation, investigate complaints, undertake research and conduct educational programs relating to human rights as set out in the International Covenant on Civil and Political Rights, the Declaration of the Rights of the Child, the Declaration on the Rights of Mentally Retarded Persons, the Declaration on the Rights of Disabled Persons and the International Convention on the Elimination of all Forms of Racial Discrimination. The commission also administers the Racial Discrimination Act 1975 and the Sex Discrimination Act 1984.

Law enforcement in Australia is handled by federal, state and territory police forces. Each is independent and all cooperate closely. The ratio of police to population nationally is about 1:550.

The Australian Federal Police (AFP) is the Federal Government's primary law-enforcement body. It has headquarters in Canberra and regional offices in each state. It enforces federal laws, including those against illegal drug importation, terrorism and breaches of currency regulations, and in Canberra it provides a full range of traditional community police services.

The AFP's officers serve in liaison posts in South-East Asia and the Pacific, Hong Kong, Singapore, Pakistan, North and South America and Britain. A contingent serves in Cyprus as part of the United Nations Peace-Keeping Force.

All states and the Northern Territory have police forces. All have specialised squads, in addition to traditional traffic and on-the-beat police, to cover specific fields — homicide, drugs, armed hold-ups and fraud. Other specialist squads are the water police and rescue squad.

Australia's police forces cooperate at various levels, notably through the Australian Police Ministers' Council, comprising all ministers responsible for police affairs. The council oversees common national police services in areas such as criminal intelligence, research and training facilities. These include the Australian Bureau of Criminal Intelligence, the National Police Research Unit and the Australian Police Staff College.

The charter of the National Crime Authority (NCA), set up in 1984, requires it to identify areas of (usually organised) crime and gather evidence to prosecute those involved. It cooperates with other law-enforcement agencies. In pursuit of a federal or state reference it has special powers, including those to hold hearings, issue subpoenas and compel witnesses to testify.

Australia has participated for decades in the international effort to curb drug abuse and trafficking. As a member of the United Nations Commission on Narcotic Drugs, it trains narcotics-control officers for countries in South-East Asia and the Pacific. In recent years the results of its efforts in this field have been very good.

Federal and state agencies such as the Australian Customs Service, the AFP, the NCA and state police forces share the task of battling illegal drug importation and trafficking. The Australian Bureau of Criminal Intelligence collects and disseminates information in this field and there is a high level of federal-state cooperation.

Government

The Commonwealth of Australia is a federation formed on January 1, 1901, of six states, by the Commonwealth of Australia Constitution Act. Each state has its own constitution and parliament and governs itself. The federal and state constitutions complement one another and the Federal Government and Parliament (a bicameral legislature having upper and lower houses) are responsible for all matters of national interest.

All states have bicameral legislatures except Queensland.

The Northern Territory and the Australian Capital Territory are also largely self-governing.

Australia is independent but retains constitutional links with Britain. Britain's monarch is also formally Australia's and is represented in Australia by the Governor-General and six state governors, each of whom is head of state and formally chief executive. The powers and duties of each include summoning, proroguing and dissolving parliament, assenting to legislation, appointing ministers, setting up government departments and appointing judges. The Governor-General is commander of the armed forces.

By convention, governors and governors-general act only on the advice of their governments on virtually all matters. They are selected by the Queen on the advice of their governments.

The Australian Constitution can only be changed by referendum and then only if a majority of voters in a majority of states, as well as an overall majority, approves. Normally, a proposal to change it must first pass each house of the Commonwealth Parliament with the support of an absolute majority of each house. However, a proposal may be submitted to the electors by the Governor-General if one house has passed it twice and the other has twice rejected it. Only eight of 42 proposals for change have been approved by referendum since 1901.

Changes to the states' constitutions do not require referendums.

A valid federal law overrides any state law inconsistent with it.

The federal houses of parliament are the House of Representatives (constitutionally the "lower" house), of 148 members, in which the majority party or coalition forms the government and selects the Prime Minister (usually from among its own number), and the Senate (the upper house), required by the Constitution to have about half the number of members of the lower house.

The lower house is elected, at least once every three years, from single-member constituencies under a preferential voting system. The party forming the government by reason of its majority in this house does not depend for its authority on a majority in the upper house. All ministers are members of parliament.

A government that loses the confidence of the lower house, by losing its party majority or otherwise, must resign or advise the Governor-General to dissolve the house to permit a general election.

Parliament House, Canberra, the national capital, is the home of federal politics

The people of each state and territory vote as a single electorate for its senators, using a proportional-representation system, and those chosen serve for either six years (for their states) or a maximum of three (territories). Territory senators' elections coincide with those of the lower house while elections for state senators are staggered so that half of them retire each three years.

The Senate's powers match those of the lower house except in relation to certain financial legislation.

Australia pioneered secret ballots in parliamentary elections and has used the system universally since 1879. Such voting is generally compulsory (although not invariably in local government elections). The franchise extends to everyone over 18 years except criminals and the insane.

There are many political parties in Australia. The largest, in no special order) are the Liberal Party, the National Party (both broadly conservative in philosophy), the Australian Labor Party (broadly socialist) and the Australian Democrats (not, by declaration, of either persuasion). All have similar structures and operate in all states and all support parliamentary democracy and its fundamentals.

Policies at the federal and state levels are decided by each government's cabinet, comprising senior ministers and the Prime Minister (Premier in the case of a state). Cabinets meet regularly in private and the only public records of their proceedings are statements by their leaders or authorised ministers. Government decisions requiring a legal basis (such as to make regulations under an existing law) require approval by executive councils, which comprise the Governor-General (or governor) and ministers.

At both federal and state levels there are career public services, most staff of which are recruited as permanent officers by open competition and win promotion on merit. Each public service is divided into departments, for each of which a minister is responsible to parliament. The head of each department, usually a career public servant, is responsible to the minister.

Departments at both federal and state level administer portfolios covering such affairs as education, the law and associated responsibilities, transport, science and technology, finance, trade, foreign relations, primary and secondary industries, tourism, health, social security and so on.

Freedom-of-information legislation came into effect in Australia in 1982, giving citizens and other accepted permanent residents freer access to certain federal government information. Its scope was widened the next year.

The functions of local government, the third tier, which generally derives its powers from state legislation, are specified normally by state legislation and vary from state to state.

Local government is financed by rates (taxes) and the state and federal governments and normally controls town planning, road construction and maintenance, water provision and wastewater disposal, building, weights and measures and other matters of local concern. Some local-government bodies operate public businesses in such industries as transport and energy.

The land

Australia is an island continent and lies between east longitudes 113° 9' and 153°39' and between south latitudes 10° 41' and 43° 39'. Almost 40 per cent is north of the Tropic of Capricorn.

On its western coast is the Indian Ocean and on its east the Coral and Tasman Seas of the South Pacific Ocean.

Its area, 7 682 300km², is about the same as the mainland United States excluding Alaska; or one and a half times that of Europe excluding the Soviet Union; or about 25 times that of Britain and Ireland; or about twice that of the combined areas of India and Pakistan.

Its coastline is 36 735km. The continental shelf extends north to Papua New Guinea and south around Tasmania, varying in width from about 30km to more than 240km. Just off the eastern coast the Great Barrier Reef extends north for 2000km from southern Queensland to the Gulf of Papua. Enclosing about 207 000km², the reef is an important marine ecosystem, a complex of islands and coral reefs containing many rare life forms.

At an average elevation of less than 300m (the world mean is about 700m), Australia is the flattest of continents. About a twentieth of it rises more than 600m.

The main structural feature, the Great Western Plateau, covers most of Western Australia, much of the Northern Territory and South Australia and part of western Queensland. Its average elevation is about 300m. Outcrops are significant mainly as geological phenomena and include Ayers Rock, a monolith 8km in circumference rising 335m above the central Australian desert.

East of the plateau, extending from the Gulf of Carpentaria in the north to eastern South Australia and the western Victorian coast, is the great lowland belt known as the Central-Eastern Lowlands. The belt's average elevation is 150m and, at Lake Eyre in South Australia, it falls to nearly 12m below sea level. These lowlands probably formed the floors of seas comparatively recently, geologically. Parts are rich in cretaceous aquatic fossils.

Rugged landscape near Alice Springs, Northern Territory

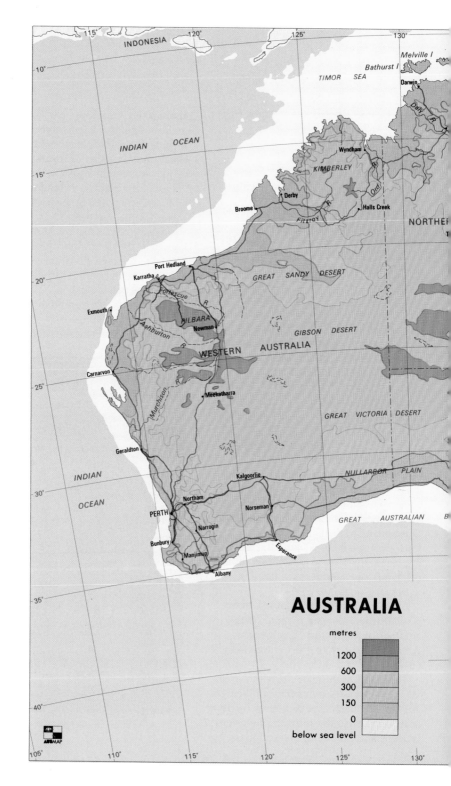

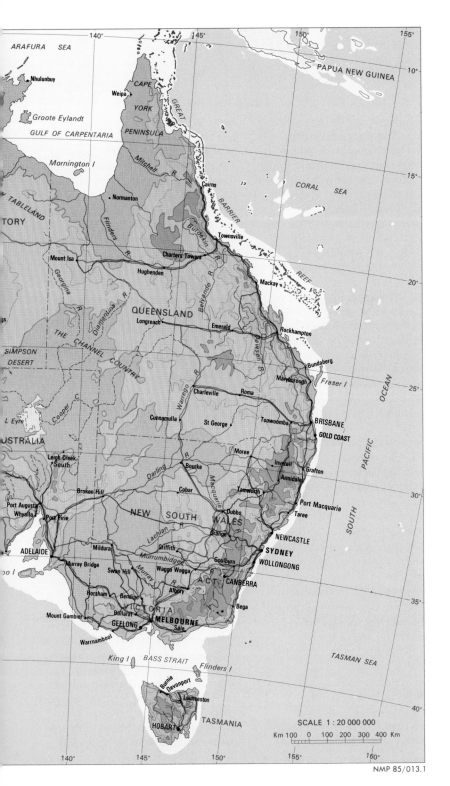

The eastern highlands, better known as the Great Dividing Range, follow the eastern coast south from far northern Queensland to southern Tasmania, never more than 400 km from the coast and sometimes forming part of it. Their average altitude is less than 910m, although peaks exceed 1800m in the rugged south- eastern area, called the Australian Alps. The Alps' highest point is the summit of Mount Kosciusko (2228m).

Nearly a third of Australia (about half of Queensland and Western Australia and most of the Northern Territory) is north of the Tropic of Capricorn and the rest is in the temperate zone. It is is less subject to climatic extremes than regions of comparable size elsewhere in the world because it is surrounded by oceans and has no extensive high mountain masses.

Clear skies and low rainfall are characteristic of the weather on most of the continent. In mid-summer (January), average temperatures range from 29°C in the north to 17°C in the south. In July, average temperatures range from 25°C in the north to 8°C in the south.

The coldest regions are the highlands and tablelands of Tasmania and the south-eastern corner of the mainland, where the only regular snowfalls occur.

Summer is from December to February; autumn March to May; winter June to August; and spring September to November. For most of the country, the hottest month is January.

Australian soils generally do not show a correlation with climate, mainly because of the persistence in certain regions of leached soils formed in earlier, wetter climatic cycles. These soils, and many in the higher-rainfall areas, are of low fertility, often needing trace elements as well as phosphorus, nitrogen and sulphur. Artificial fertilisers can allow these soils to support highly productive pastures which have potential for mixed farming. Research for tropical pastures is being done on the leached, porous yellow and red earths and grey and brown clays in northern Australia.

The sub-humid and semi-arid zones have large areas of less-leached and more-fertile soils such as red-brown and black earths, which are important to Australia's wheat industry. Seventy per cent of the continent is arid, so the better-quality soil types are grazed extensively.

Australia is the driest inhabited continent and its rainfall varies extremely in both the geographic and seasonal senses. Mean annual rainfall is 465mm. Rainfall varies from less than 150mm over the centre of the continent to more than two metres in parts of the tropics and western Tasmania. The average annual surface runoff, about 440km^3, represents only 12 per cent of total rainfall. Evaporation accounts for most of the rest.

As a yardstick: Africa's annual runoff is 18 times Australia's (38 per cent of total rainfall); Europe's nearly six times Australia's (39 per cent); Asia's about 30 times Australia's (48 per cent) and North America's 16 times (52 per cent).

The continent's interior has few permanent watercourses. More than half the nation's runoff is from drainage regions remote from the major population centres. The Murray River and its tributaries are Australia's largest system, having a catchment of 1.06 million square kilometres in southern Queensland, New South Wales and

Tropical beauty of Lawn Hill Gorge, Queensland

Victoria. Most of Australia's irrigated land is in the catchment and 60 per cent of exploitable surface water is committed.

The system's runoff, 22 700 million m³, is small by world standards. The largest, the Amazon, has more than 250 times the runoff; the Congo about 60 times; the Yangtze 48 times; the Brahmaputra 26 times and the Mississippi 25 times.

Groundwater lies under most of the continent but in varying quantity and quality. Much of the inland depends on it for stock and domestic consumption. The largest such resource, the Great Artesian Basin, is of 1.7 million km², mainly in Queensland and New South Wales.

Three-quarters of the water Australia uses irrigates 1.5 million ha of agricultural land and eight per cent goes to stock and rural domestic use. About a fifth is for urban, including industrial, purposes.

In recent years, natural and irrigation-induced salinity in water tables has reduced water quality in important areas and there has been increasing emphasis on research to reverse these effects.

The native forests of Australia are hardwoods and occur mainly in the wetter coastal belts. The coexistence of rainforests and sclerophyll forests, unrelated botanically, is an ecological curiosity. The best-known native trees are the gums (eucalyptus, about 550 species) and wattles (acacia, 600 species). Wattles are akin to North America's and Europe's mimosa. Gums range in size from the 90m mountain ash to stunted arid-zone types. One, the jarrah, is one of the world's hardest and most durable woods.

Many of Australia's fauna are unique — some even grotesque compared with those of the Old World. Their evolution, influenced by factors not present elsewhere, seems to have been unaffected genetically by outside influences because of the geographic isolation of their home.

About half the native mammals are marsupials (they keep and suckle their immature young in pouches) although a few have no pouches. Mammals include the kangaroo, koala, wombat, dingo, possum, dugong (aquatic), echidna (spiny ant- eater) and platypus. The latter two are monotremes, which both lay eggs and suckle their young. The first platypus seen in England (a dead one sent back by a scientist) was regarded as a hoaxer's jest; the platypus has fur, a duck-like bill and four webbed feet (two with spurs). It is amphibious.

About 530 of Australia's 700 bird species are considered native. They include the emu, lyrebird, bower bird, kookaburra (which has a song like an uninhibited laugh), bellbird and whipbird. Most of the world's parrots are Australian natives. There are many hawks and eagles.

Despite diligent efforts over two centuries, some scientists believe that there are still hundreds of Australian native creatures to be identified formally and catalogued.

Koala at rest

Kangaroo on alert

Saltwater crocodile suns itself

The arts

Many aspects of the arts in Australia have their roots in Europe, but Australia's own history and culture and the influence of its Asian neighbours have made an impact. Distinctively Australian trends are developing, and the vigour and originality of the arts in Australia often surprises visitors.

In the late 1970s and early 1980s the great problem facing the arts was one familiar in other nations — rising costs and a decline in government financing — but increasing public interest provided the momentum to carry them through difficult times. The Australian Government's funding agency for the arts is the Australia Council, which spends more than $50 million a year. More is spent by state governments.

The Australia Council boards support specific art forms and central council programs support research, education, multicultural arts and other "trans-art-form" areas.

A big role in music and drama is played by the federally-funded Australian Broadcasting Corporation. State governments and municipal councils also support the arts.

Australian painting developed distinctive characteristics toward the end of the 19th century in the work of such artists as Tom Roberts and Frederick McCubbin.

Several living Australian painters have world-wide reputations. In recent years the names of John Olsen and Brett Whiteley have been added to the longer-established names of Sidney Nolan, Arthur Boyd and Albert Tucker. More sculptors, painters and craftspeople are living by their creativity than ever before.

The Australian National Gallery in Canberra is known worldwide for its collection of Australian art, particularly Aboriginal art. The National Gallery of Victoria holds works by Rembrandt, Titian, Tiepolo, Turner, Rubens, Van Dyck, Reynolds, Gainsborough, Corot, Modigliani and Pissarro. The Art Gallery of NSW in Sydney has a representative collection of works by Australian painters and sculptors. Another important Sydney gallery is the Power Gallery of Contemporary Art.

Several valuable art awards are offered in Australia, including the annual Archibald Prize for portraiture, the Wynne, Sulman and Blake prizes, and the annual Britannica awards. Business organisations have sponsored many travelling exhibitions and are important buyers of Australian works.

The Sydney Biennale is now part of the international art calendar and Australian artists participate in biennales, exhibitions and arts festivals in other countries.

The Visual Arts/Craft Board of the Australia Council makes direct grants to help artists and craft workers and helps them indirectly via commissions, acquisitions, exhibitions and artist-in-residence projects. It also encourages a greater awareness of contemporary Australian works and helps across the artistic spectrum.

The crafts flourish in Australia; increasing numbers of people make a living from them and people can work toward a career in crafts just as in any other branch of the arts. The Visual Arts/ Crafts Board encourages improvement in the quality of crafts, provides greater opportunities for craftspeople to further their professional development, fosters wider community access to the crafts and assists in creating an awareness of Australian crafts overseas and of work from other countries in Australia. Special attention is given to training and workshop experience, and increasing contact between craftspeople and community groups.

Artbank was established in 1980 to stimulate a wider appreciation of Australian art and to help Australian artists by buying their works, which it hires out to government offices, overseas missions and corporate clients.

The Federal Government also encourages major foreign and Australian touring exhibitions of art and cultural property.

After a promising start in 1896, the Australian film industry experienced widely varying periods of prosperity and popularity in the early 1900s and 1940s.

Since 1969, it has had a resurgence, Federal Government support providing the mainspring. In 1973, the Australian Film, Television and Radio School was established. Trainees and graduates have had a significant impact in all areas of film and television production. Two years later the Australian Film Commission

Aboriginal artists, Dan Tjungurray and Paddy Carroll Tjungurray

was created to support development and encourage distribution and broadcasting of film productions. It makes grants and loans for these purposes and has a special fund to help innovative and less commercial projects and new talent. In 1981 the Government introduced generous tax concessions to encourage private investment in films and in 1988 established the Australian Film Finance Corporation to provide the industry with direct support by equity participation.

Australia's history of film, television, radio and recorded sound is reflected in the National Film and Sound Archive's vast collection of films, television productions, photographs, posters, sound recordings, radio programs, equipment and other related materials. Its collection ranges from what is believed to be the world's first feature film, *The Story of the Kelly Gang*, made in 1906, to contemporary works. The sound collection covers the earliest music cylinders, such as recordings of Nellie Melba and Peter Dawson.

The country found its first lyric poet in Henry Kendall, who wrote of the gentler aspects of the Australian landscape. Kendall's contemporary, English-born Adam Lindsay Gordon, was the forerunner of the school of bush balladists, including A.B. "Banjo" Paterson and Barcroft Boake.

Some of the early traditions of Australian writing were born of the work of Henry Lawson, whose poems and ballads had wide popular appeal. Between the wars Kenneth Slessor introduced into Australian poetry the English modernism of T.S. Eliot. He was followed by others who looked to their native roots for inspiration.

Since World War II, writers have been concerned with social problems and universal themes and a lively school of contemporary experimental stylists has emerged.

The short story has always played a significant part in Australian literature. Henry Lawson was acclaimed for his poetry but it was his short stories which most clearly depicted the Australian's relationship with his environment. Among prominent present-day writers are Frank Moorhouse, James McQueen, Peter Carey, Michael Wilding and Vicki Viidikas.

Lawson was followed by many social-realist writers, including Joseph Furphy, Vance Palmer, Katharine Susannah Pritchard, Xavier Herbert, Dymphna Cusack and Kylie Tennant.

In fiction, the convict and bushranger novels of Australian writers Marcus Clarke (1846–1881) and Rolf Boldrewood (1826–1915) have been followed by many books diverse in period, style and subject. Their authors include Henry Handel Richardson, Louis Stone, Patrick White, Hal Porter, Dame Mary Gilmore, Thea Astley, Thomas Keneally and Peter Carey (1982 and 1988 Booker Prize winners), Morris West, Colleen McCullough, Elizabeth Jolley, David Malouf, Beverley Farmer and Kate Grenville.

Australia has strong traditions in children's literature and some of the most prominent modern writers are Ivan Southall, Patricia Wrightson, Colin Thiele and David Martin.

The Literature Board of the Australia Council encourages creative writing by making grants to writers and by subsidising publication of their works.

The Government funds the Public Lending Right Scheme to recompense authors and publishers for the use of their books by public lending libraries.

The National Library of Australia holds millions of books and more than 100 000 titles of periodicals and newspapers from many parts of the world and an extensive microfilmed collection of rare and significant printed items. Its departments cover oriental studies, music manuscripts, maps, rare books, pictorial history (paintings, drawings, prints and photographs), area studies, oral history and films. It operates extensive computer services, including the Australian Bibliographic Network.

Australia has eight large professional orchestras, six of which — one in each state capital — are run by the Australian Broadcasting Corporation (ABC). The Elizabethan Philharmonic Orchestra in Sydney and the State Orchestra of Victoria work with the Australian Opera and the Australian Ballet. The ABC Sinfonia trains postgraduate musicians for a career in the symphony orchestras.

The Australian Opera (AO), based in the Sydney Opera House, is the national opera company. Some states have small professional opera companies. The AO tours regularly and also reaches wide television and radio audiences.

Musica Viva Australia operates one of the largest ensemble music concert networks in the world. In addition to its main concert series of international groups and artists, it organises overseas tours for Australian ensembles and commissions works by Australian composers.

Jazz musicians are receiving more grants and commissions, and jazz-group tours are included in Musica Viva's program. Australian pop artists are well known internationally.

The Performing Arts Board of the Australia Council extends opportunities for musicians, to stimulate composition and to encourage diversity in music training, and supports many performing companies. Distinctive Australian drama is written by playwrights such as David Williamson, Dorothy Hewett, Jack Hibberd, Alex Buzo, Barry Oakley, John Romeril, Stephen Sewell, Steve Spiers and Louis Nowra.

The board and state governments support regional and community theatres and smaller companies which work mainly in schools or community venues. Commercial theatre organisations are important in the country's theatrical life.

The National Institute of Dramatic Art, Australia's major theatre school, has about 120 students in acting, technical production and design. There is a one-year postgraduate directors' course.

The national ballet company, the Australian Ballet, tours state capitals, while regional companies supported by state governments and the Australia council perform mostly in their own capitals and provincial centres. The Council also promotes the development of dance, drama, puppetry, mime and youth theatre.

In recent years, Aboriginal arts have attracted unprecedented attention and consolidated their position in the Australian arts spectrum, stimulated in part by official encouragement. Much of this encouragement has been channelled through the Australia Council, which helps Aboriginal communities to maintain and develop traditional cultural

Australian Ballet's Lisa Pavane as Nikiya and David McAllister as Solor in "La Bayadere"

activities, and generate new artistic expression. The Australian National Gallery has been instrumental in changing perceptions of Aboriginal Art from primarily anthropological to artistic.

The Community Cultural Development Committee of the Australia Council helps foster broader community involvement in the arts, responding to ideas that involve arts activities in a community context. It favours programs initiated in the community that reflect local needs and interests and demonstrate community support and participation in decision-making and activities.

The number of museums in Australia has increased dramatically in recent years, reaching more than a thousand. Many use new display techniques, which are attracting increasing numbers of visitors.

Owned by the Commonwealth and states, regional authorities and private individuals, they acquire and preserve Australia's cultural heritage including, among many more specialised classifications, works of art, documents and scientific and historical material.

The most important of the nationally owned museums are the National Museum of Australia, the Australian National Gallery, the National Library of Australia, the Australian War Memorial, the National Film and Sound Archive and the National Science and Technology Centre, all located in Canberra, and the Australian National Maritime Museum, in Sydney.

Australia has legislation designed to protect its most important cultural heritage material from indiscriminate export. This law also provides for protected objects, obtained illegally in foreign countries and imported to Australia, to be returned.

The people

Australia's population, about 17 million, occupies a 7.7-million- square-kilometre continent, giving the impression of extremely sparse settlement — two people to the square kilometre.

In fact, only 15 per cent of Australians live in rural areas. The vast majority live in the cities and the bulk of the population is in the south-eastern corner, as much of the rest of the continent is too rugged or arid for close settlement.

The population has more than doubled since 1945 and much of the increase has resulted from a migration program so vigorous that today about a quarter of the population is foreign-born. Both net migration and natural increase began falling sharply about 20 years ago.

Culturally, Australia is part of the West; its lifestyle is like those of Western Europe and North America.

Most members of the labour force work for wages or salaries, generally five days a week, and have a month's paid leave and about 10 paid public holidays a year. Most people retire at the age of 60 or 65.

The "average" Australian female lives for 78 years and her male counterpart for 72. Most Australians marry in their late 20s.

Couples have 2.1 children. Most couples own or are buying houses, all but a few have refrigerators and colour television sets and most have telephones and at least one car (about a third have two). Nearly half have freezers; one-fifth have dishwashers.

There is one chance in three that the male in the household will have a trade certificate or tertiary qualification and about one in five in the case of the female. Women comprise about 40 per cent of Australia's total workforce. In the 1980s, the average annual household income reached about $30 000.

European settlement devastated the Aboriginal population of Australia. Not much more than a century after the first Europeans arrived, the Aboriginal population had fallen to about 70 000 — the lowest it reached. This figure is approximate and depends on such factors as the then official definition of an Aboriginal, the reliability of the censuses

Enjoying a picnic on Sydney Harbour foreshores

and official knowledge of the existence of remote tribal groups.

The 1986 census results were that there were nearly 228 000 Aboriginals and Torres Strait Islanders, 68 000 more than five years before.

This apparently startling population growth rate is explained mainly by the fact that, in 1986, more people of Aboriginal descent chose to identify themselves as such, and also by the fact that more effort was devoted in 1986 to obtaining reliable figures in this category. There was also some natural population growth.

Modern Australia's efforts to encourage Aboriginal self-determination is based on making their participation in decision-making as wide as possible. The Australian Government helped set up the National Aboriginal Conference (NAC) as a forum for Aboriginal views and policy development at local, state and national levels. The NAC advises the Government on long-term goals and programs to achieve them, and reviews existing programs' effectiveness. The Aboriginal Development Commission (ADC) was set up in 1980 to further the economic and social development of Aboriginals.

Four million migrants from most parts of the world have arrived since World War II, when the population was 7.4 million. The largest source has been Britain, and Europe, Asia and Oceania are the main regional sources. The largest intake was 185 000 in 1969–70. Many Asian newcomers are Indo-Chinese refugees.

Migrants are accepted who have close family ties in Australia; capital and business expertise; skills, qualifications or

A cooling swim on a summer day

Sailing is a popular recreational activity

to help migrants adjust to their new country.

A free telephone interpreter service operates 24 hours a day and there is another service to translate documents relating to individuals' settlement. Many federal departments provide interpreting and translation services to inform settlers about government matters and some issue information documents in many languages.

Each year, substantial numbers of students are brought to Australia for long-term formal education and specialised training.

Australian citizenship can be acquired by birth in Australia, by being born of an Australian parent outside Australia, by grant, or by adoption in Australia on or after November 22, 1984. It is not acquired automatically by someone who marries a citizen.

Foreigners who have settled permanently in Australia may be granted citizenship after two years' residence if they have a basic knowledge of English, know enough about the responsibilities and privileges of citizenship and are of good character.

There is no discrimination on the basis of sex, marital status, national origin, race or religion and the law provides for appeals against decisions to deny or remove citizenship.

About three-quarters of Australians profess Christianity. Of these about a third are Catholics and another third Anglican. Many non-Christian faiths are followed including Judaism, Buddhism and Islam. Australia's tradition of religious tolerance is evidenced by a wide distribution and variety of places of worship.

qualities needed in Australia; or refugee status. Others qualify under special humanitarian programs.

A party to the UN Convention and the Protocol Relating to the Status of Refugees, Australia has long been seen as a haven by many of the world's persecuted and dispossessed. It maintains its traditional humanitarian stance on refugees, who are selected individually from all parts of the world. Increasing attention is being paid to Latin America, the Middle East and Africa as well as eastern Europe and Indo-China.

Of 11 000-plus refugees accepted in 1986–87, about half were from Asia, which brought Australia's total refugee intake since World War II to nearly half a million.

Australia's adult-migrant education program includes English classes and a range of courses, services and programs

Science and technology

The need to improvise and innovate in pioneering days nurtured an interest in research and invention that has grown into a vibrant scientific and technological community.

Australia's progress in technology and the natural and social sciences has been rapid since World War II and has accelerated sharply in the last two decades. Significant advances have been made in water research, specialised surgery, veterinary medicine and nuclear-waste disposal.

Progress in technology and the natural and social sciences has been rapid since World War II and has accelerated sharply in the last two decades.

Much of the Australian Government's research funds are spent in its own agencies — notably the Commonwealth Scientific and Industrial Research Organisation (CSIRO), the Australian Nuclear Science and Technology Organisation, the Department of Science, the Institute of Marine Science and the Department of Defence — but large sums go also for research in universities, research institutes, industry and the like. Most state-government funding for research and development is spent within state agencies, mainly to advance agriculture and mining.

For many decades the country's reputation for innovation was based on advances in agriculture, mining, science and medicine but, in recent years, it has widened to embrace other fields. More recent developments have been as diverse as an internationally accepted aircraft-landing system, a vastly superior diamond-tipped cutting tool and a way to mass-clone genes for cancer research.

They derive from a research base that is sound by any standard, and a national technology strategy designed to make the country's manufacturing and tertiary industries technologically competitive. Its goal is to strengthen all aspects of Australia's science and technology and its thrust is three-pronged — research and development, education and training, and technological exchange and interaction.

A Commission for the Future works to raise community awareness of the social and economic impacts of technological change, particularly in areas some people, especially the unskilled, see as threatening — robots, computers, artificial intelligence. A corollary of the threat is addressed also: the availability of jobs in a technological society.

The Federal Government is encouraging the development of a high-technology industry sector based on research in such fields as biotechnology. It gives high priority to promoting business-funded research and development, particularly in the manufacturing, service and information industries. It funds the Australian Industrial Research and Development Incentives Board's grants program and has enhanced the financing capacity of the Australian Industry Development Corporation for export and technology. It funds fellowships to place post-doctoral researchers in industry and has a scheme to place young graduates in industry to help integrate university and industry research.

Its own major research facilities — in the higher education system and the CSIRO — are available to industry, and 150 per cent of expenditure on research and development (not otherwise funded by Government) is tax-deductible. A Federal Government department is responsible for coordinating technology policy.

State governments also encourage high-technology industries.

The CSIRO is Australia's main scientific research body. Its program covers all fields except defence, nuclear energy and clinical medicine and it employs about 7000 people in about 100 laboratories and field stations. Divisions are grouped into institutes that concern themselves with the needs of major industry and community sectors — animal production and processing; industrial technologies; information and communications technologies; minerals, energy and construction; natural resources and the environment; and plant production and processing. CSIRO collaborates with industry in joint research and commercial ventures to introduce new technology in Australia.

The Australian Centre for Remote Sensing receives and processes data from the Landsat series of earth-resources satellites and also from the Japanese marine observation satellite MOS1 and the French earth observation satellite SPOT. It has a data-receiving station at Alice Springs, in the centre of the continent, and a processing centre in Canberra to convert the data into photographs and computer-compatible tapes for analysis by resource managers worldwide.

CSIRO scientist develops pollution-fighting bacteria

The Australian Space Office manages — for the US National Aeronautics and Space Administration (NASA) — the Canberra Deep Space Communication Complex (space tracking station), at Tidbinbilla in the Australian Capital Territory, and its mobile laser tracking facility at Yarragadee, Western Australia.

The NASA space tracking stations in Australia have supported virtually all NASA non-military space missions and those launched by NASA for other countries. They have played a major communications role in the manned landings on the moon, the manned Skylab earth-orbiting space station, the Viking project in search of life on Mars, the Voyager missions to the outer planets, and space-shuttle missions.

The Tidbinbilla station tracks and communicates with spacecraft on planetary and interplanetary missions, earth-orbiting scientific satellites and space-shuttle missions and the laser tracking facility provides voice links with space-shuttle astronauts as well as tracking laser-reflecting satellites.

The joint geological and geophysical research station at Alice Springs, managed jointly by the Federal Government and the US Air Force, is one of several such stations in the world which monitor the limited test-ban treaty to which the Australian and US governments are signatories.

In the Antarctic and sub-Antarctic, Australia maintains scientific stations at Mawson, Davis, Casey and Macquarie Island, organises annual Antarctic expeditions and conducts research in Antarctic marine science, cosmic-ray and upper-atmosphere physics, glaciology and biology and investigations in medical science. Australian research organisations also conduct programs there in the Southern Ocean. Australia cooperates with nations active in the Antarctic Treaty.

The Bureau of Meteorology operates the World Meteorological Organisation's Melbourne world weather watch centre — the other two are in Moscow and Washington — and a regional centre in Darwin. The centres collect and analyse data and make their information available to all countries requesting it.

The Patent, Trade Marks and Designs Office, with about 22 million patent documents from many countries, has offices in all capitals and acts as an international searching and preliminary examining authority under the Patent Cooperation Treaty.

The Australian Nuclear Science and Technology Organisation (ANSTO), a statutory body, helps develop Australia's uranium resources and its use of various forms of nuclear energy. ANSTO's research establishment, the major centre for peaceful nuclear research in Australia, is part of the Lucas Heights Research Laboratories, about 30km south-west of Sydney, NSW. It operates Australia's two nuclear reactors, used only for research.

Major parts of the research program are projects on the impact of uranium mining on the environment, the use of radio-isotopes to study hydrology and sedimentation, the immobilisation of radioactive wastes in SYNROC, waste repositories and radionuclide migration, the medical applications of radio-isotopes and radiation, radiation biology, industrial applications of radio-isotopes and radiation, radiation sterilisation and disinfestation of foods, radiation standards, nuclear safeguards, fusion, and a range of underlying research and scientific services.

ANSTO has a strong commitment to international collaboration, technical assistance, training, and commercial services (mainly sales of radioisotopes). It supports the Australian School of Nuclear Technology and collaborates with most Australian universities through the Australian Institute of Nuclear Science and Engineering.

More than 200 technical and professional associations and societies are involved in the development and organisation of specific sciences. The Australian Academy of Science is the senior national institution covering the physical and biological sciences.

Formal bilateral agreements exist between Australia and the US, India, the Soviet Union, the Federal Republic of Germany, China, Japan and Mexico. A

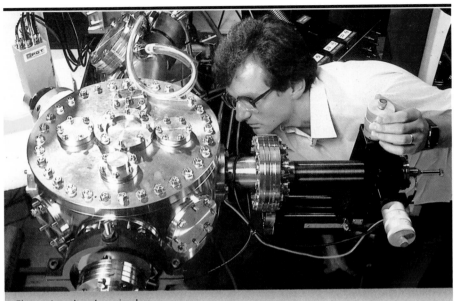

Electronmicroprobe analyses mineral ore

scientific exchange program exists between the Australian Academy of Science and the Academia Sinica of Beijing.

The 3.9m Anglo-Australian telescope, one of the world's largest, operates at Siding Springs Mountain, NSW, and, with the associated laboratory in Sydney, is used for original investigations in astronomy and astrophysics.

The Australian National University in Canberra operates telescopes at Siding Springs Mountain and at Mount Stromlo, near Canberra. Mount Stromlo has 10 instruments, of which the largest telescope is the 1.9m reflector, used mainly for spectroscopic investigations. Siding Springs has 2.3m and one-metre telescopes, a 40cm reflector and a 60cm reflector designed for studying starlight polarisation.

The Australia Telescope was inaugurated in September, 1988. It consists of a 64m-diameter steerable parabolic reflector near Parkes, NSW, six steerable and moveable 22m antennas at Culgoora, NSW, and a steerable antenna at Siding Springs.

Used to study radio emissions from Milky Way galaxy objects and to observe many galaxies beyond, it is run as a national facility by a team supported by CSIRO through its Division of Radiophysics.

The Parkes dish has operated in its own right for many years. It relayed the images of man's first steps on the moon and, in 1986, supported NASA's Voyager fly-by of Uranus and the European Space Agency's Giotto satellite encounter with Halley's Comet. In August 1989 it helped Voyager again in its fly-by of Neptune.

Transport and communications

Among the most daunting challenges Australia presented to its inhabitants was the creation of efficient transport and communications systems.

Without both, the nation's political and commercial viability would never have matured; but Australia's size, almost empty interior and small population made their creation difficult, slow and expensive.

They were created, however, and rank now with those of other industrialised nations.

On a tonne-kilometre basis, road, rail and coastal shipping share domestic freight almost equally. On tonnage alone, however, road transport carries nearly 80 per cent. Passenger travel, too, is dominated by road.

Australia's transport system includes nearly 840 000km of roads, 240 000km of unduplicated air routes and 40 000km of government railways.

The Federal Government owns a number of major transport and communications businesses: Qantas, the national overseas airline, and Australian Airlines, the domestic one; the Australian National Line (shipping); Australian National Railways; Telecom (internal telecommunications); OTC Limited (overseas telecommunications); AUSSAT Proprietary Limited, which administers the nationally owned space satellite system, AUSSAT; Australia Post and the Federal Airports Corporation.

From the late 1980s, programs have been under way to improve the efficiency and commercial performances of all these enterprises. They include processes of deregulation.

Australia's overseas trade is served mainly by foreign-flag vessels, most of them bulk carriers. Although liner shipping carries only a very small proportion (by weight) of goods, its share by value is more than a third of total exports.

The largest Australian-flag operators are the Australian National Line (ANL) and the Broken Hill Proprietary Company (BHP). The ANL operates 14 vessels (10 in the overseas trade) and BHP 17 vessels, 11 in the overseas trade.

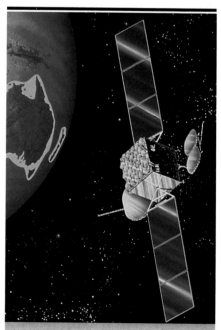

New AUSSAT satellite to be launched in 1991

Australia has about 70 ports of commercial significance. The main ones serve state capitals and industrial and mining centres.

The Federal Government is responsible for operational and regulatory maritime matters for shipping in the international and interstate trades, oil-pollution control and the safe construction, crewing and operation of ships. It also provides marine navigational aids and co-ordinates maritime search-and-rescue services.

Australia's railways are mainly government-owned and-operated. States have their own systems. The Australian National Railways Commission, a statutory authority, operates non-urban services in South Australia and Tasmania.

The railways' main tasks are to haul long-distance freight, bulk minerals (particularly coal in Queensland and NSW), grain and petroleum products, and to carry suburban and inter-urban passengers.

Three gauges are used: 1067mm, 1435mm and 1600mm, but the mainland capital cities are connected by a standard-gauge (1435mm) line, except for Adelaide- Melbourne. Each state has privately owned railways serving mining, agricultural and industrial areas. The largest serve iron-ore mining developments in the north-west of Western Australia. Queensland has an extensive tramway network to supply mills in sugar-producing areas.

Australian roads are funded approximately equally by all three tiers of government. The 16 000km National Highway System, which links all capitals, is a federal responsibility.

Federal road programs have been funded since the early 1980s from the excise levied on petrol and diesel fuel. More recently, additional funds have been allocated to the states and territories for public transport, road safety research and rail systems.

In 1988, there were three road deaths for every 10 000 registered vehicles in Australia. This index has declined by more than two-thirds from the 1960 figure, 9.3. The 1988 total was 2888 deaths. That year was the eighteenth consecutive one in which the total number of deaths had remained below the 1970 peak, despite a population increase of 2.1 million and growth by 4.1 million in the number of vehicles.

Trucks carry about four-fifths of domestic freight. The trucking industry is diverse and very competitive, comprising small and large operators using vehicles ranging from small vans to road freighters and "road trains" — articulated trucks with one or more trailers.

Regulation of trucking operations is primarily a state responsibility. The Federal Government helps to develop co-ordinated transport policies and uniform approaches to the fostering of safety and responsiveness to economic and social needs.

Transport uses about three-quarters of all vehicle fuel. Since 1979, incentives have been offered for the conversion of vehicles to liquefied petroleum gas, and many government and private fleet vehicles have been converted, particularly taxi-cabs.

Federal authorities are responsible for promoting safety and efficiency in civil aviation, traffic control and navigation networks at airports, airworthiness regulations and negotiating air traffic agreements with other countries.

Thirty-six international airlines, including Qantas, operated regular services to Australia in 1988–89. They were: Aerolineas Argentinas, Air Caledonie International, Air China, Air India, Air Nauru, Air New Zealand, Air Niugini, Air Pacific, Air Vanuatu (operated by Australian Airlines), Alitalia, All Nippon Airlines, British Airways, Canadian Airlines International, Cathay Pacific Airways, Cook Islands International (operated by Polynesian Airlines), Continental Airlines, Flying Tigers (cargo only), Garuda Indonesian Airways, Hawaiian Airlines, Japan Air Lines, JAT Yugoslav Airlines, KLM, Lauda Air, Lufthansa German Airlines, Malaysia Airlines, Merpati Nusantara Airlines, Olympic Airways, Philippine Airlines, Polynesian Airlines, Royal Brunei Airlines, Singapore Airlines, Solomon Island Airlines (operated by Air Pacific), Thai Airways International, United Airlines and UTA French Airlines.

Qantas operates a fleet of 25 Boeing 747s and 11 Boeing 767s (at 30 June 1989) to 23 countries. Qantas services operate to 10 Australian airports — Adelaide, Brisbane, Cairns, Darwin, Hobart, Melbourne, Perth, Port Hedland, Sydney and Townsville.

It carries more than three million passengers a year to and from Australia — more than 40 per cent of the total carried by all airlines serving Australia. Australia has air-service arrangements with 34 countries.

Scheduled domestic airlines carry about 13.5 million passengers a year, representing about 13 250 million passenger-kilometres a year.

Maintaining national airline QANTAS aircraft

There are 430 licensed aerodromes used for civil operations in Australia. Twenty-three, including those in the major capitals, are controlled by the Federal Airports Corporation (FAC). Forty-four are owned and controlled by the Federal Government.

The major internal airlines are Australian Airlines and Ansett Airlines of Australia, the chief operating division of Ansett Transport Industries Limited, a diverse company engaged in tourism, road and air travel, freight, hotels, manufacturing and television. Other Ansett-owned airlines operate regional services throughout the country.

Australian Airlines operates on all main interstate routes and on intrastate routes in Queensland. It owns Australian Regional Airlines Pty Ltd and has a major interest in Eastern Airlines Pty Ltd.

Between them, the major internal airlines have 108 aircraft — three Airbus

A300s, three Airbus A320–200s, a Boeing 727–100, 21 Boeing 727–200s, 30 Boeing 737–300s, five Boeing 767–200s, 15 Fokker F28s, 11 Fokker F27s, 10 Fokker F50s, five DC9s and four BAe 146s.

The approximately 50 commuter operators in the Australian aviation industry use about 220 aircraft with 38 or fewer seats or payloads up to 4200 kg and about 240 airports. They carry about 1.3 million passengers a year.

There are about 900 commercial operators using 8267 aircraft. General aviation includes all non-scheduled operations, such as charter, training, agricultural and other specialised work.

Communications

The main communications systems — posts, telegraphs and telephones — were established by the colonial governments and are now operated by businesses owned by the Federal Government. The first postal service began in NSW in 1809 and the first telegraphic service in 1854. Four years later, Sydney, Melbourne and Adelaide were linked by telegraph. Sydney and Brisbane were linked in 1861. In 1878, two years after Bell invented it, the telephone was introduced in Australia.

Postal, telegraph and telephone services became a national responsibility in 1901 when the colonies federated. Responsibility for them is vested in four corporations owned by the Commonwealth Government.

Australia Post (the Australian Postal Corporation) employs about 35 000 people and handles about 10 million postal articles a day.

Telecom Australia (the Australian Telecommunications Corporation), employs more than 90 000 people and operates more than seven million telephone services, most through automatic exchanges. Direct subscriber dialling accounts for most outgoing overseas calls. There are large networks of telex, data, value-added, facsimile, broadband and mobile-telephone services.

Telecom's network of large-capacity broadband trunk systems uses microwave radio, coaxial cables and optical-fibre transmission systems.

OTC Limited controls telephone, telex, telegram, facsimile, leased circuit, audio broadcast, electronic mail and data transmission, which are by submarine cable, satellite and short-wave radio. Television relay and video-conferencing are by satellite. OTC also controls communications with ships at sea.

OTC is the world's third-largest investor in, and user of, INTELSAT. Through OTC, Australians can use the world's largest direct-dialling telephone network for access to nearly 200 other countries.

AUSSAT Proprietary Limited owns and operates the Australian National Satellite Communications System. It is extending and improving communications around Australia and providing high-quality radio and television services to remote areas and neighbouring regions. Three identical satellites form the first-generation system and will be replaced, in time, by a second generation of two upgraded satellites.

The economy

The complexion of Australia's economy has changed in less than 50 years from one which relied mainly on primary production to a mature, diverse one in which nearly three-quarters of production is in the services (tertiary) sector.

The demands of World War II and a strong postwar immigration program spurred a rapid expansion of secondary industry, diversification and overall economic growth. At the same time, massive investment occurred in export-oriented mining and energy projects.

Although rural industry accounts for only a small fraction of Australian production, its exports compose about a third of total exports. Australia leads the world in wool production and is a major supplier of wheat, meat and sugar.

In the mining sector, too, production is a small part of the total but energy and mineral products account for more than a third of total exports. Australia is one of the world's largest coal exporters and a major supplier of iron ore, gold, bauxite and alumina.

This heavy reliance overall on mining, energy and agricultural exports sets the Australian economy apart from almost all other Western economies.

Australia has shared with other industrialised countries relatively high inflation and unemployment rates since the mid-1970s. An admixture of fiscal and monetary policies with a carefully developed prices-and-incomes policy and continuing structural reforms have had significant success against both problems.

After growing at solid rates in the late 1970s and early 1980s, the Australian economy fell into recession in 1982–83. Since then it has been generally buoyant and has had strong increases in both output and employment.

Australia has a central wage-fixing system. From 1983 to 1986 the wage-fixing principles provided for wages and salaries to be indexed to movements in the Consumer Price Index. Since then they have been linked with improved efficiency and productivity and involve the removal of restrictive work and management practices and other institutional barriers to labour-market flexibility.

The centralised system is part of a Prices and Incomes Accord reached in 1983 by the Federal Government and the Australian Council of Trade Unions, providing for a wages-and-taxes trade-off resulting in improvements in real disposable incomes and, at the same time, moderated increases in labour costs.

The Prices Surveillance Authority was established in March 1984 as part of the prices and incomes policy. Its function is to encourage price restraint to match wage restraint. It concentrates on areas in which effective competition is lacking and in which price or wage movements are pervasive in the economy, an approach which recognises that competition is usually an effective constraint on price.

In late 1989 the Commonwealth Government created the Industries Commission as an independent analytical body to advise it on, among other things, the need for structural change. The Government's broad objective was to make the best use of the nation's resources and expand its productive potential. Its terms of reference cover many aspects of Australia's important industries.

Over the 1980s, Australia's current-account deficit averaged 4.5 per cent of gross domestic product, about twice the average of the previous two decades.

This was the result of high domestic demand (relative to that of the rest of the world) and a lack of international competitiveness because of high inflation and inflexible labour markets in the early 1980s; depreciation of the Australian dollar between 1984 and 1986, which increased interest and dividend payments abroad; and the collapse in 1985-86 of the terms of trade, which decreased export receipts relative to import payments.

Australia took firm action to remedy these problems and improvements continue to be apparent.

Most exchange controls were abandoned by Australia in 1983 in line with the decision to "float" the $A. The value of the $A, expressed in $US, fell sharply from mid-1984 to a low of 57.95 US cents in July 1986. Despite occasionally quite severe fluctuations, it rose again fairly quickly and has remained broadly stable (generally at or above 75 US cents for several years.

Australia's foreign-investment policy seeks to encourage long-term direct foreign investment consistent with the community's needs. The Foreign Investment Review Board examines proposals for new-business establishment involving investments of $10 million or more, takeovers of Australian businesses with assets of $5 million or more and most real-estate acquisitions. In all but a few sectors the guidelines for approval are quite liberal.

Foreign investment is restricted to varying extents in civil aviation, the media, banking, uranium and developed residential real estate. Australian equity-participation guidelines (50/50) apply to new projects in the non-oil and non-gas mining sector and to acquisitions of developed commercial real estate. The guidelines are administered flexibly.

The Federal Government presents its Budget in August each year to cover from July 1 of that year to June 30 of the next.

Federal Government outlays represent about a quarter of Australia's gross domestic product, while state, territorial and local government outlays represent about a fifth. Because of transfers between these sectors, public-sector outlays as a whole represent about a third of GDP. Excluding transfers to other levels of government, the Commonwealth accounts for about half of total outlays.

About three-quarters of total public-sector revenue is raised by the Federal Government. More than a quarter of total outlays are payments to state, territory and local governments and half of these consist of untied budgetary assistance. The vast bulk of this assistance varies in per-capita terms from state to state, recognising differences in their revenue-raising capacities and their costs of providing services.

The remainder of federal payments to the states and territories are for specific purposes such as education, health, housing and transport. The states raise about half their revenue from their own sources, mainly from taxes and other charges.

Local-government outlays are equivalent to about two per cent of GDP. About three-quarters of local-government revenue comes from the sector's own sources (mostly property rates and taxes). The rest is transferred from the federal and state governments.

The federal and state governments are members of the Australian Loan Council, which co-ordinates all government and semi-government borrowings. All forms of such borrowings have "global" limits, reached by negotiation within the Loan Council.

Taxes are levied at all levels of government. The division of taxing powers stems from the Constitution and arrangements made in response to economic and social factors.

Only the Federal Government can impose customs and excise duties, including most forms of general sales taxes. All other types of taxation are available also to the states but in practice there is little duplication. For nearly half a century only the Federal Government has levied income taxes on companies and individuals. The states' revenue comes from such levies as payroll tax, taxes on property and financial transactions, motor-vehicle and franchise taxes and financial assistance from the Federal Government.

Australia has comprehensive agreements for the avoidance of double taxation with Britain, the US, Canada, New Zealand, Papua New Guinea, Singapore, Japan, the Federal Republic of Germany, the Netherlands, France, Belgium, the Philippines, Switzerland, Malaysia, Sweden, Denmark, Ireland, Norway, the Republic of Korea, Malta, Italy, Finland and Austria. Agreements with other countries are negotiated continually and come into force from time to time. Limited agreements dealing with airline profits have been concluded with France, Italy, Greece and India.

The banking system comprises the Reserve Bank of Australia (the central bank) and 35 banks or banking groups operating under its supervision. Some banking services to corporate and commercial customers are also provided by about 120 money-market corporations (which are also known as merchant banks and include a large number of subsidiaries of foreign-owned banks), and by other non-bank financial institutions including finance companies,

Fuel tax is a revenue source

pastoral companies and general financiers. Household customers can have transaction and savings accounts not only with banks but with building societies and credit unions, and flexible investment vehicles for household savings are available also through insurance companies and cash management trusts.

The Reserve Bank's functions and powers are similar to those of other central banks. It regulates the monetary and payments system, manages the note issue, performs banking and other services for the government, and acts as banker to the banks.

The Australian financial environment has undergone considerable change in the 1980s as the Government progressively removed regulatory controls over financial intermediaries. These steps included the floating of the exchange rate of the Australian dollar in December 1983; the abolition of exchange controls; the removal of controls on interest rates on bank deposits and lending; the authorisation of 16 new foreign-owned banks, including subsidiaries of many of the world's leading banks; and the removal of restrictions on foreign participation in non-bank financial intermediaries. As a result of deregulation and changes in technology and customers' attitudes, the activities of banks and other categories of financial institutions overlap extensively.

Deregulation has allowed the domestically owned banks to compete more effectively with more specialised non-bank financial institutions, and to extend their operations internationally in competition with foreign banks. The range and volume of financial services available to both business and household customers has increased considerably.

Financial deregulation and technological developments have prompted a number of changes in the stockbroking industry.

In April 1987 the six major capital-city stock exchanges merged into a single national stock exchange, the Australian Stock Exchange Limited (ASX). Each became a subsidiary.

The ASX has responsibility for listings on its main board while the subsidiaries have retained responsibility for listings on their secondary boards.

The ASX has created a National Guarantee Fund out of the subsidiaries' fidelity funds. The fund provides for increased investor protection by guaranteeing transactions on the exchange and by compensating investors for losses resulting from defalcation or insolvency of stock-exchange members.

These developments have produced a more efficient framework for trading securities and raising capital in Australia. They have also facilitated the introduction of technological innovations in securities trading and settlement of transactions.

Insurance

Life-insurance companies, through premiums paid on policies and by interest earned on accumulated funds, account for substantial savings each year.

Tourism

A series of geological and historical accidents has made Australia one of the world's most attractive countries from the tourist's viewpoint. The vast movements of the earth's crust made it large, isolated it and positioned it across the tropical and temperate climatic zones. Among the results are a small population, which has left enormous areas unspoiled; an astonishing variety of environments, from desert to rainforest, from tropical beach to snowfield, from big, sophisticated cities to vast uninhabited areas; a wide array of unique and intriguing animals and flora; a comfortable and sunny climate; and an interesting, cosmopolitan and friendly people.

Many of its world-renowned attractions are specific, if large, like the Great Barrier Reef, Ayers Rock, and Kakadu National Park; others are general, like its thousands of kilometres of superb beaches and large skiing resorts.

Tourism is the largest industry in Australia, representing about six per cent of the gross domestic product and providing, directly or indirectly, more than 400 000 jobs.

More than two million tourists visit Australia each year, spending about $3500 million.

Australian promotes itself as a tourist destination through offices in Auckland, Chicago, Frankfurt, Hong Kong, London, Los Angeles, New York, Osaka, Singapore, Tokyo and Toronto.

Nearly 840 000km of roads make most of the continent accessible by surface vehicle. Domestic airlines link the cities, towns and resort areas. Major centres are connected by 40 000km of railways.

The two major domestic airlines have "See Australia" fares that offer substantial savings to visitors travelling on return international promotional fare tickets.

Trains are modern and air-conditioned and have sleeping compartments, dining and lounge cars. The rail system includes some of the best long-distance passenger trains in the world.

Coach companies offer tours ranging from the camping variety to those involving full (in many cases, luxurious) accommodation and from part of a day in one locality to weeks, covering much of the continent. Express coaches commute between capital cities and major towns, many as feeder services to the air and rail networks. Passes are available enabling low-cost travel on national networks. Car-rental companies deliver to airports, hotels and motels.

Notes for visitors

There are official tourist offices in all capitals and some regional centres, providing a full range of usual services for visitors. Many smaller towns have their own such offices.

Entry requirements for tourists are as simple as possible, but all visitors except New Zealand citizens must have visas and all must have current passports, valid for three months longer than the intended stay. Applications for visas can be made at Australian Government offices overseas. A return or onward-

passage ticket or evidence of enough funds for the period of intended stay may be required. On arrival in Australia, visitors are asked to produce completed incoming passenger cards (which are usually distributed aboard aircraft and ships), passports and visas. Visitors may not take jobs or enter formal studies and are expected to leave at the end of their authorised stays.

A wide range of hotel, motel and apartment accommodation is available in most cities and major resorts and many rural areas. There are also camping parks, many with on-site caravans or cabins. Hotel and motel rooms normally have telephone, private bathroom, television, refrigerator and tea- and coffee-making

facilities. Check-out time is usually 10am-11am. The main difference between hotels and motels in Australia is that hotels must provide a public bar. "Private" hotels and guest houses do not have permits to serve liquor. Many country properties offer holidays which include participation in farm activities. Tourist offices provide details and can arrange bookings.

Visitors tend to underestimate distances and travelling times in Australia. Australia is 25 times the size of Britain and Ireland combined and examples of its longer distances are: Perth to Sydney (3315km — 3 hr 55 min by air); Brisbane to Darwin 2887km (3 hr 45 min) and Melbourne to Perth 2871km (3 hr 40 min).

Darling Harbour, Sydney, is a popular venue for residents and visitors alike

A yellow-fever vaccination certificate is required from travellers one year of age and over coming from infected areas.

Visitors can bring their personal effects into Australia without paying duty, including, for those 18 years old and older, 250 cigarettes or 250g of cigars or tobacco and one litre of alcoholic liquor, provided it is carried with them. Dutiable goods to the value of $400 ($200 for visitors aged under 18), included in personal baggage, are also duty free.

Quarantine: Australia is free from many insect pests and diseases, so the importation of fruit, vegetables, seeds, animals and plants or animal or plant products is controlled strictly. The interiors of all aircraft arriving in

Australia from overseas are sprayed to control flying insects which could introduce diseases.

Post offices are generally open from 9am to 5pm Monday to Friday. Stamps are often available at front desks of hotels and motels.

Australia has a modern automatic telephone system.

Shops are generally open from 9am to 5.30pm weekdays and from 9am to noon Saturdays. Most shops are closed on Sunday. Some cities have night shopping on specific days of the week and on Saturday afternoons and, in major tourist centres and resorts, it is common for shops to be open at night, on holidays and at weekends.

Getting away to a remote river

There is variety of restaurants to suit all tastes and pockets, from top-class restaurants with international cuisine to small coffee shops serving snacks. All cities have a range of restaurants of virtually every ethnic origin. Virtually all restaurants have liquor licences — "full" (permitting the storage and sale of liquor) or "BYO" ("bring your own"). Some provide for both.

Standards of hygiene are high in the preparation of food for sale to the public and tap water is safe to drink in any Australian town. Fresh food is plentiful at shops and markets. Sea foods and all meats, fresh fruit, salad and vegetables are of high quality and quite safe to eat. Australian wines and beer compete with considerable success in international markets.

Australia uses the metric system of weights and measures. Speed and distance are in kilometres, goods in kilograms and litres, temperature in Celsius (the same scale as Centigrade).

Australian currency is decimal: 100 cents = $1. No other currency is legal tender. Exchange facilities are available at international airports, banks and major hotels. Current exchange rates are available from banks. Travellers' cheques (ideally in Australian dollars) are accepted at banks and major hotels. Their acceptance elsewhere depends on the policy of the individual trader.

Bank trading hours vary, but banking facilities are usually available from 9.30am to 4pm Monday to Thursday and 9.30am to 5pm on Friday. The commonly accepted international credit cards include American Express, Diners Club, Carte Blanche, Visa and MasterCard.

No service charges are added to accounts by hotels or restaurants. Tipping is neither encouraged nor routine, although visitors may reward special service if they wish, in which case 10 per cent of the bill is adequate. At any time, tipping is optional. Taxicabs and porters have set charges and do not expect to be tipped.

The electrical current in Australia is 240/250 volts AC, 50 cycles. The Australian three-pin plug is unlike those of many other countries' (and is extremely safe) and adaptors are usually required for shavers or hairdryers. However, universal outlets for 240V or 110V shavers are usually available in leading hotels.

Visitors may bring up to four weeks' supply of prescribed medications. For larger quantities, a doctor's certificate is needed. It is wise to carry a doctor's prescription which, on endorsement by an Australian doctor, will permit a pharmacist to provide further supplies in Australia.

Visitors who are covered by Australia's national health-insurance scheme, Medicare, are those who are residents of one of the five countries with which Australia has reciprocal health-care arrangements — the United Kingdom, New Zealand, Italy, Malta and Sweden.

Before leaving Australia, every person over 12 years of age must pay a $10 departure tax (exemptions apply to 48-hour transit passengers and some multi-departure passengers). Departure-tax stamps are bought at airports with Australian currency or by American Express, Diners Club, Visa, Mastercard or Bankcard.

Social services

Australia has a well-earned pioneering reputation in social services.

Its action in 1909 — only eight years after federation — in funding pensions for the aged, was radical at the time, as were similar pensions for invalids, introduced the following year and, only two years later, maternity allowances (an early attempt to encourage population growth).

The main components of today's social-security programs are pensions for the aged, invalids and sole parents; unemployment, sickness and special benefits; additional amounts for children; sheltered employment and rehabilitation allowances; and allowances for families with children. Such social-security and welfare programs account for about a quarter of GNP. They are non-contributory and usually paid direct to the recipient. The emphasis is on income support, based on need. Eligibility for most pensions depends on an income or means test.

Voluntary organisations are important adjuncts to welfare schemes. Traditionally, charitable organisations have supplemented social services, often as pioneers.

The Federal Government helps people whose source of income has ceased, because of invalidity or retirement, for example, or has been interrupted by unemployment, sickness and the like. Most payments are made under the Social Security Act from consolidated revenue. Administrative and capital costs are paid from separate annual appropriations.

Age pensions are paid to people of limited means; men must be at least 65 and women 60. Invalid pensions are payable to people aged 16 and over who are permanently incapacitated to a specified degree. The spouse of either class of pensioner may be eligible for a pension if he or she is not otherwise entitled to one.

A sole parent's pension is available to single people caring for children under 16 years of age or children entitled to the child-disability allowance. A pension is also available to certain older women who are widowed or divorced. Income and assets tests apply to those seeking age, invalid and sole parents' pensions.

People who qualify for pensioner concessions are entitled to free

Care and facilities for the disabled

pharmaceuticals and some optometrical services. Concessions on government transport fares and telephone rental are available. Other concessions vary from state to state.

A family allowance is paid to eligible parents or guardians with one or more children who are under 16, or are full-time students aged between 16 and 25 and not receiving an education allowance. Families with very low incomes may receive a supplement.

Pensions for war/defence widows comprise a basic pension and domestic allowance. Payments to each dependant are paid without a means or assets test.

Free hospital, medical, dental, optical and legal services are also available to such widows and their dependent children.

A child-disability allowance is payable to parents or guardians of a child whose physical or mental disability requires constant care and attention in the family home.

Benefits are available to people who, through unemployment, sickness or injury, are temporarily unable to work.

A discretionary payment (called a special benefit) may be made to people who are not eligible for other forms of assistance and are not able to support themselves.

Disabled people employed in sheltered workshops may be paid an allowance equal to the invalid pension.

A mobility allowance may be paid to disabled people who are employed or engaged in training and are unable to use public transport because of their disabilities.

Social workers and welfare officers are located in nearly 200 regional offices.

Aboriginal liaison officers and welfare officers are employed to work with Aboriginal communities and organisations. Migrant services units across Australia monitor and review services to migrants and refugees and liaise with ethnic and voluntary groups.

Grants are made also to non-profit community-welfare agencies so they can give emergency relief by cash or food vouchers. Non-profit organisations and local-government bodies may receive grants for providing accommodation.

The federal and state governments fund jointly a wide range of welfare services based on home care for aged and disabled people and families.

About 1500 nursing homes and 1000 hostels receive federal financial support, to provide residential care for frail aged people. About a fifth of these are state-operated nursing homes.

The Federal Government's Disability Services Program funds organisations to provide services that will help people with disabilities maintain their independence and achieve their full potential. Services include competitive employment training and placement, supported employment, respite care, accommodation support, recreation, advocacy and information.

The Commonwealth Rehabilitation Service employs teams of medical specialists, therapists, trade instructors, teachers, social workers and vocational counsellors to work with disabled people, without charge, to help them return to economic and social independence.

Sport

Almost all Australians, regardless of social position, income or age, have a sporting interest of some kind, and the variety of such interests available to them is extremely wide. It can be anything from a full-time occupation for an Olympics-bound athlete, through a weekly social cricket match, to watching horse races on television.

Australia has more than 130 national sporting organisations and thousands of state, regional and club bodies. More than half the population, according to an authoritative estimate, is registered to participate in sports. Many more indulge in non-competitive activities like fishing, bushwalking, boating, horse riding and fitness programs.

Children lean mainly toward cricket, swimming, Australian Rules football, baseball, rugby, netball, softball, soccer, hockey, basketball and tennis. Australia's Little Athletics organisation has 70 000 members aged between five and 12 years.

About a million girls and women compete regularly in various sports and there has been a sharp increase in recent years in organised events for older competitors.

Watching also qualifies as a form of sport. It is common for more than 100 000 people to attend the grand final of the Australian Rules club competition in Melbourne and large numbers in all cities, all year round, watch major sporting events.

Although Australia did very well for decades in international competition without the sophisticated training techniques available in countries in which athletic endeavour was heavily supported financially, its approach to competitive sport has changed in recent years.

On one hand, governments have taken a much larger hand in the development of sporting expertise and encouraging the talented and, on the other, there has been a spectacular increase in commercial sponsorship.

This has stemmed largely from increased television coverage of sport and has prompted sponsors to increase prize money. In total, businesses are investing many millions of dollars a year in direct subsidies and as much again in promotion, marketing and other support.

Australian Rules football draws big crowds

Athletes compete in international trials

Cricket, football, tennis and racing have benefited most. Prizemoney for the Melbourne Cup, Australia's richest horse race, reached $1 million in 1985. Ten years earlier, it had been $156 700. Commercial sponsorship for many sports, and at most levels, has also increased sharply.

The Federal Government has a ministerial portfolio specifically concerned with sport and, through it, allocates large sums to its development.

In 1980 it established the Australian Institute of Sport and, four years later, the Australian Sports Commission. The institute, its headquarters in Canberra, has a large staff including highly qualified specialised coaches. It has more than 300 students in many disciplines, including basketball, diving, gymnastics, hockey,

netball, rowing, soccer, squash, swimming, tennis, track and field, water polo and weightlifting. It has specialised outrider units in several states.

The institute's headquarters are integrated with Canberra's National Sports Centre, which has world-class facilities including a 25 000-capacity stadium, a 5000-seat indoor arena and major facilities for many Olympic sports, both indoor and outdoor. The 1985 Athletics World Cup was held there.

The Australian Sports Commission (ASC) is an independent body funded by the Federal Government. It coordinates sports development policies and programs in Australia and its main objectives are to sustain and improve Australia's level of achievement in international sporting competition and to increase the level of participation in sport by all Australians. The commission is responsible for administering the Sports Development Program, one of the most important continuing government support schemes for sport.

The National Sports Facilities Program encourages construction of modern sports facilities throughout Australia. It is funded on a dollar-for-dollar basis by the federal, state and territory governments.

Other programs funded by the ASC include:

• The National Coaching Accreditation Scheme (NCAS), aimed at increasing the proficiency of coaches by introducing uniform standards of instruction for each sport.
• Aussie Sports, designed to offer children in their last three years of primary school the opportunity to build a wide base of basic sports skills by experience. Involving children in more than 30 modified sports, such as Kanga Cricket and Minkey (hockey), it had reached more than 500 000 children by the end of the 1980s.
• The Disabled Sport Program (DSP), which funds national sporting organisations for the disabled in a way comparable to that in which organisations for able-bodied people are funded through the Sports Development Program. DSP also provides funds to promote integration of sporting activities for able-bodied and disabled people. Its objectives are:
  — to encourage people with disabilities to participate in sport and to provide them with opportunities to do so at their desired level and to achieve their personal goals regardless of sex, race, age or level of disability; and
  — to encourage the integration of sporting activities of people having disabilities with those of the able-bodied.
  — The Women's Sport Promotion Unit (WSPU), established by the ASC to promote women in sport and promote sport to women.
  — The Anti-Drugs Campaign, which discourages the use of drugs in sport to create a fair, competitive sporting environment in Australia.

The campaign maintains close liaison with international organisations to ensure a unified approach. It involves a program of independent testing of athletes during training and at competitions.

The National Sports Information Centre collects and disseminates Australian and overseas sporting information of value to athletes and coaches, sports science and sports medicine specialists, sport administrators and the general public.

State governments provide strong financial support for sport at state and club levels in two main categories — facility development and sports development. These funds are used to hold state titles, in coaching and administrative training schemes, to supply equipment, in school and junior coaching clinics, and in specialised coaching for individual athletes. State funds also help send teams to Australian championships.

Although the Australian Government generally welcomes and encourages sporting contact with other nations, it has signed the Gleneagles declaration and will not allow tours by teams and individual amateurs from South Africa.

Visits by Australians to South Africa for sport are discouraged.

Australia allows visits by Taiwanese sporting teams, groups, individual and sports officials on the basis that they are representatives of Taiwan Province.

Local, state and national sporting associations undertake responsibility for the development of sport at each level. This includes conducting competitions, developing coaching, and selecting and training representative teams.

National organisations established to administer specific aspects of sports development comprise representatives of state organisations and include the Australian Olympic Federation, the Australian Commonwealth Games Association, the Australian Sports Medicine Federation and the Australian Council for Health.

Physical Education and Recreation.

Most national sporting organisations are affiliated with the Confederation of Australian Sport, a national forum, while the Sport and Recreation Ministers' Council (SRMC) is the main mechanism for liaison between governments on these matters. Its membership is apparent from its name.

Australia has long participated in international sport and has built a fine record, particularly when the size of its population and its geographic remoteness from other centres of competition are considered. It is one of only three nations (Britain and Greece are the others) to have competed at every modern Olympics and has competed in all 12 Commonwealth Games. It hosted the 1956 Olympics and the 1938, 1962 and 1982 Commonwealth Games. Australians have won 67 Olympic gold medals, mostly in swimming, and 304 in Commonwealth Games.

The country's enormous coastline and numerous waterways are used by swimmers, surfers, 150 000 competitive yachtsmen and large numbers of power-boat enthusiasts, and surfboard and sailboard riders. Most Australians learn to swim before they are 10 years old. A survey indicated a few years ago that fishing — including underwater fishing — was Australia's most popular outdoor activity. Australia has more than 1000 public swimming pools and probably more than a million private ones.

If swimming has done most to bring Australia international sporting acclaim, tennis is its nearest rival. Squash, cricket, golf, rugby, hockey, netball and track and field follow. Between 1950 and 1969, Australia won the Davis Cup 15 times, and again in 1973, 1977 and 1983. Between 1952 and 1971, Australian men won the Wimbledon singles title 14 times and Australian women won the women's singles five times between 1963 and 1980.

Horse racing was one of the first sports properly organised in Australia. The first official race was run near Sydney in 1810, only 22 years after the first colony was established, and the Sydney Turf Club was formed 15 years later. Today, racing is extremely popular and a major industry. The Melbourne Cup, a handicap race over 3200m, is the country's richest race and best-known sporting event, having been run every year since 1861 — which makes it the oldest event on Australia's calendar. The day on which it is run, the first Tuesday in November, is a public holiday in

Thoroughbred horseracing is a popular sport

Melbourne, and work ceases throughout Australia when the horses jump at 2.40 pm.

Gambling on horse racing is heavy and is done through on-course bookmakers and off and on course through the Totalisator Agency Board. The board's turnover exceeds $4000 million.

Cricket is Australia's most played and watched summer team sport. It has an estimated 500 000 registered players. Test matches and one-day internationals played between teams of Commonwealth nations sometimes attract crowds of 80 000. The game in Australia underwent a revolutionary change in 1977 when a commercial organisation, World Series Cricket, entered full-scale promotion of international matches (in opposition to the Australian Cricket Board). It signed most top Australian cricketers as well as leading players from Pakistan, England and the West Indies. Some of its innovations were immediately successful and have been retained, including games under lights, coloured clothing and white balls. After two seasons, the promoter withdrew and the board once again controls all first-class cricket.

Australians play and watch four codes of football — Soccer, Rugby Union, Rugby League and Australian Rules, a game devised and played only in Australia (although it is similar in some respects to Irish Football). It is the most popular code in Victoria, Western Australia, South Australia, Tasmania, southern NSW, the Australian Capital

Territory and the Northern Territory. Perhaps 500 000 people play the fast-moving game and it attracts far more spectators than any other event. Soccer (460 000 registered players) gained in strength and popularity with the post-war influx of European migrants and since 1977 has had a national league. Rugby Union (100 000 players) and Rugby League (154 000) have their strongest following in NSW and Queensland. Australia is generally considered the world's leading Rugby League nation and it is ranked highly in Rugby Union.

Most of Australia's population lives within 100km of the coast and there has always been a keen interest in sailing. Australian designers have created several internationally recognised classes of craft, including the Australia-type catamaran and the Australian 18-footer, one of the fastest and most exciting open racing yachts in the world.

The nation's international yachting reputation leapt when, 1983, Australia II became the first foreign yacht in 132 years to win the America's Cup. Australia first accepted the America's Cup challenge in 1962 and has engaged the United States in most of the finals since then.

The most famous yachting event on the Australian calendar is the Sydney-to-Hobart race, which has been run annually since 1945. It is a handicap race over 630 nautical miles and attracts entries from many parts of the world. Australia's yachtsmen compete regularly in the Admiral's Cup at Cowes, Britain, and have won twice — in 1967 and 1979.

The diversification of Australian society in the past 50 years has stimulated interest in a wide range of other sports,

Disabled athletes compete

including basketball, baseball and volleyball, bocce (so soundly transplanted from Italy that Australia hosted the world titles in 1981), orienteering, ice hockey and, in the high country in the south-east corner, alpine and cross-country skiing attract about 300 000 regulars.

Australian disabled athletes are making their presence felt internationally sportscene, and performed exceptionally well at the 1984 International Games for the Disabled, held in the USA and Britain, winning 46 gold medals, 54 silver and 47 bronze and setting 30 world records. The Federal Government provided substantial funding to assist the Australian team prepare for and compete in these games.

The media

Most Australians have daily contact with the mass communications media — newspapers, magazines, radio and television.

Research shows Australians read more newspapers per head of population than any other nationality, and as a result, newspapers in the nation's capital cities enjoy large circulation figures.

There are two national daily newspapers — *The Australian*, printed simultaneously in Sydney, Melbourne, Brisbane and Perth, and *The Australian Financial Review*.

Each state capital has at least one morning and one afternoon daily newspaper (Sydney has three morning and one afternoon). While carrying national and international news, there is a strong local identity in their news coverage. There are also many suburban weeklies in the capital cities. Larger regional cities have daily newspapers while smaller population centres are served by weekly newspapers. All told about 600 newspapers are published in Australia, more than half of them outside the capitals.

Australia's oldest newspapers are: *The Sydney Morning Herald*, 1831; *The Herald* (Melbourne) and *The Geelong Advertiser* (Victoria), 1840; *The Examiner*, (Launceston, Tasmania), 1842; and *The Mercury* (Maitland, New South Wales), 1843.

There is a flourishing periodical press with large circulation: general and women's-interest magazines, business and specialty magazines covering almost every interest. An active foreign-language press caters to settlers of many different origins. There are 150 publications in about 40 languages.

Most major newspapers are owned by a small group of proprietors for whom print-media interests are only part of larger and diverse business empires. Changes to legislation governing media ownership introduced cross-media legislation which prevents owners of radio and television stations from owning another media outlet in the same market.

Radio and television

Radio and television broadcasting services are provided by national, commercial, multicultural and public organisations.

National (non-commercial) services are provided by the Australian Broadcasting Corporation (ABC), a nationwide radio and television service. The ABC has an overseas service, Radio Australia. The Special Broadcasting Service (SBS) provides non-commercial, multilingual radio and multicultural television services and financial and program support to public broadcasters presenting multilingual programs. The ABC and SBS are solely responsible for their program material.

Most of the ABC's capital and running costs are funded by the Federal Government, which makes an annual budget contribution of about $500 million. The ABC supplements its budget through the sale of its programs domestically and abroad; book, cassette and record sales; and publication of three monthly magazines.

There are ABC symphony orchestras in all six states and a national training orchestra, the Sinfonia, making the ABC the world's largest entrepreneur in the orchestral field. It runs concerts featuring local and overseas artists.

The ABC's radio and television programs range through music, news, light entertainment, drama, documentaries, rural, religion, children's and education programs. It maintains a nationwide independent news service producing and broadcasting 100 000 radio bulletins and 5900 TV bulletins a year. It has its own journalists in all capital cities and major regional cities and in 15 cities in 12 other countries.

Radio Australia is the international shortwave service of the ABC. It broadcasts in English 24 hours a day and for varying periods in Indonesian, Mandarin, Cantonese, French, Japanese, Neo-Melanesian (Pidgin), Thai and Vietnamese.

Commercial radio and television stations operate under licences from the Australian Broadcasting Tribunal. The tribunal has powers to hold public inquiries into the granting, renewal and transfer of commercial and public broadcasting licences as well as into such matters as setting standards of broadcasting practice. The tribunal is assisted by the Children's Program Committee made up of people with expertise, background or interests that enable them to advise the tribunal on programs suitable for "C" classification and inform the industry and public about developments in children's television. The Australian Broadcasting Tribunal has quasi-judicial powers.

There are more than 170 commercial radio stations, most broadcasting on the AM band and a growing proportion — now about a quarter — on the FM band.

Australia's public broadcasting stations are non-commercial, catering for education, community or special interests. More than 70 such stations are on the air, nearly all on the AM band. They obtain their funds from a variety of sources, including government grants, public subscription and sponsorship announcements.

Commercial television began in Australia with Sydney commercial station TCN9's regular transmissions in 1956. Now there are more than 250 stations and hundreds of relay stations.

Formal regulation is confined to:
• licensing radio and television stations;
• limiting the degree of ownership or control individuals or corporations may aggregate;
• setting standards governing the proportion of advertising;
• classifying films and television programs;
• setting the proportion of local content, including advertising, to guarantee a reflection of the Australian way of life and promote employment opportunities for Australian writers, artists, producers and others dependent on the broadcasting industry.

Although major newspapers, radio and television networks maintain overseas news bureaus in many parts of the world, the leading source of overseas news for the Australian media is Australian Associated Press (AAP) which has been a part owner of the international newsagency Reuters since 1946. AAP's Sydney headquarters has satellite,

Producing a television commercial

appearing and/or named in the courts.

The Australian Press Council sets out ways of dealing with breaches of ethical standards of the press in its booklet *Aims, Principles, Constitution and Complaints Procedure*. The council has an independent chairman, 11 industry members, one editorial member not allied to any publishing group, two journalist members and eight public members.

The council has no legal powers and is financed by contributions from its constituent bodies. The council also reviews developments likely to restrict the supply of information of public interest and importance; reports publicly on developments in press ownership and control; publishes statistics and makes representations to governments, public inquiries and organisations in Australia and overseas on freedom of the press.

Australia's journalists, artists and photographers in print media, radio and television are members of the Australian Journalists' Association (AJA). Many members also work in government departments and in public relations firms. The AJA represents them industrially and oversees compliance with its code of ethics, breaches of which may lead to stringent penalties.

microwave and cable links with the world's major news centres. Its national communications network includes telegraphic data, microwave and news picture circuits. It receives the news services of Reuters, Associated Press, Agence France-Presse, Press Association of Britain, *New York Times* and *Chicago Daily News*. It has domestic news-gathering bureaus in all state capitals, Canberra and Darwin, and bureaus in London, Wellington, Port Moresby and Jakarta.

There is no media censorship other than a system of "D-notices" which media proprietors have agreed to observe on matters affecting national security. The main restraints on publication are the laws of libel and other laws and regulations protecting the authority of the courts and the rights of those

Index